America Branding in the Digital Age

How I Grew from Zero to One Million Followers in A Year with Social Media Marketing While Creating A Business Identity that is Contagious

Wyatt Croasdell

Contents

Chapter 1:
The Importance of Personal Branding _____ 1

Chapter 2:
The Future of Branding is Personal_____ 12

Chapter 3:
Designing a Purposeful Personal Brand _____ 16

Chapter 4:
Social Media and Personal Branding_____ 21

Chapter 5:
Creating a Personal Brand on YouTube _____ 33

Chapter 6:
Creating a Personal Brand on Facebook _____ 55

Chapter 7:
Creating a Personal Brand on Twitter _____ 72

Chapter 8:
Creating a Personal Brand on Instagram_____ 92

Chapter 9:
How to Capitalize on Personal Branding_____ 118

Chapter 10:
Google Search with Personal Branding SEO _____ 132

Chapter 11:
Powerful Personal Branding Secrets _____ 143

Chapter 12:
Become the Next Million Dollar Brand _____ 148

Chapter 1:
The Importance of Personal Branding

"Personal branding is about managing your name — even if you don't own a business — in a world of misinformation, disinformation, and semi-permanent Google records. Going on a date? Chances are that your "blind" date has Googled your name. Going to a job interview? Ditto."

– Tim Ferriss

The term 'personal branding' is steadily becoming an integral part of society. There are lots of reasons for this change, and most of these reasons are beneficial to an individual. To fully grasp the concept of a personal brand, there are various aspects you need to consider. In this chapter, you will get a clear picture of what personal branding means and why you should create your personal brand now.

What Is A Brand?
If you perform a quick Google search to get the answer to this question, you will get so many results and it could become overwhelming.

However, there are simple ways to define a brand to make it understandable to anyone.

A brand is a word or term associated to a company or individual that indicates the unique aspects of the services or products they offer to differentiate them from similar services or products that another company or individual is offering to the same consumer. How an individual picture your business is your brand.

Branding, on the other hand, can be defined as the process of creating a unique personality that your consumers can attribute to your business.

What Is A Personal Brand?

A personal brand is a form of identity that you create for yourself as an individual. It is the image you want the world to remember any time they see your name, product, or services. As an identity, it consists of the attitudes, conduct, words, and behaviors that your customers have come to expect anytime they get in contact with you or your business.

With so many individuals running similar businesses or offering the same services, a personal brand helps create a unique persona that differentiates you from the other businesses. A personal brand can be for your own private use or for professional reasons.

The growth of a personal brand can either be controlled or organic. A controlled method of growth involves taking strategic steps to develop the image you want your customers to have about you and your business. The organic growth of your personal brand doesn't include any strategic action and can sometimes be a very chaotic growth.

Personal branding is a process that has evolved over the years. Before the advent of the Internet, people had to make business cards to tell others about themselves. The media also played an essential role in making it possible for several individuals to become known around the world. Nowadays, all you need to build your brand is access to social media.

Why Do You Need A Personal Brand?

There are lots of reasons why you should create a personal brand today. Creating a personal brand is a way of exposing yourself to the limitless opportunities that are available. As a professional running a business or searching for a job, a personal brand can connect you to your next big client or introduce you to your potential employer.

Taking control of your personal branding ensures that the image that these individuals have of you is positive and not an image that can be detrimental to your career in the long run.

Through a personal brand, you can showcase your passion, strengths, and get people to believe in you as an individual. You can also establish yourself as an authority through the personal brand. If people get to know more about you, it becomes easier for them to believe in what you have to say. Building trust in today's world doesn't have to involve meeting up with an individual in person.

Clear indications of the power of personal branding are evident in how social media influencers effortlessly sway the decisions of their followers. It is also the same for celebrities that have built a fan base.

Why Is Personal Branding Your Key to Success?

If you want to be successful in whatever you do, having a personal brand is crucial. It is merely what you need to stand out in the large crowd. For any skill you develop, a personal brand can help you establish yourself as an expert.

According to recent statistics, a lot of companies are moving from traditional marketing methods to social media marketing strategies (Chen, 2019). This means that more people are listening to social influencers. Personal branding makes you an influence over your audience.

If you run a small business, a personal brand can be pivotal to the growth of the business. Unlike with a larger company, it is not easy to differentiate the owner of a small business from the business itself. Creating a personal relationship with your customers through your personal brand will make it easy to sell your products and services to these customers.

Laws of Branding

When branding yourself or a business, there are specific laws you must follow to ensure that you are doing it in the right way. Depending on how you go about your personal branding, you may ruin your image permanently. Below are the laws you should commit to memory when creating your brand.

Leadership

Leadership from a branding perspective is how you establish the expertise of your brand within an industry. Becoming a leader through your brand will involve becoming an authority through your knowledge, skill, and by earning the respect of other brands, as well as individuals.

Visibility

The most successful personal brands are those that can get in the view of the target audience regularly at different periods. Your visibility depends on how well you can network the brand. If no one hears about your brand, you won't be getting any potential customers to search for the brand.

Personality

Your personal brand is all about your image. Who are you? How would others describe you? In creating a personality for the brand, you need to use yourself as the basis.

What unique traits do you possess? What are the flaws that make you who you are?

Specialization

It is the process of narrowing the focus of your brand to a specific area. In personal branding, it is what results in niche selection. You should not create a personal brand to meet the demands of everyone in an industry. Find a focused area of the industry where your skills or services will be in high demand.

Distinctiveness

A personal brand should be unique. The unique features of the brand are those minor traits that make the brand memorable to all your customers. These traits should be easy for the customers to recollect a long time after they interact with the brand.

Persistence

A personal brand will not become successful in one day. It requires time to reach its full potential. It is also crucial that you have a strategy in place to guide the growth of the personal brand. Having a set of values is also vital.

All these are necessary to avoid straying away from the goal you want to achieve. It is easy to change your values when you look at the current trends online. If you must change values regularly, it becomes difficult for people to connect with your brand.

Goodwill

Your brand will grow in its influence if your customers can perceive the brand to have a good intention towards them. Your goal is to build a brand that people can respect, appreciate, and trust.

Utility

A personal brand reflects who you are as an individual. Everything your personal brand stands for should be who you are as an individual.

After interacting with your customers, you want your reviews and feedback to mention that as an individual, your personality aligns with the personal brand your customers have come to love.

The Benefits of Having A Personal Brand

There are various rewards you can enjoy when you take active control of your personal brand. It makes you a self-reliant individual and promotes your growth in other aspects of life.

For an in-depth look at some of the benefits of a personal brand, read on below.

To Promote Trust

Building a personal brand helps you define your intentions. These intentions appear in a genuine and well-detailed manner which are some of the essential qualities you need to develop trust in another individual.

If people have an idea of what you are going to do next and know the extent you are willing to go, they will feel at ease when working with you.

It Helps to Grow Your Connections

Personal branding is one of the best ways to connect with other individuals within an industry or an area of expertise. Personal branding can be both online and offline. The essential part of the personal branding goal is to develop a reputation that is known to various individuals.

Through the reputation you gain from personal branding, it becomes easy to get a spot as a speaker at an industry event. These events are often the best places to connect and network with other like-minded people. Depending on the kind of individuals you meet, you can also generate leads from various events.

It Boosts Your Credibility

If people can recognize your name within the niche you decide to set up your personal brand, it becomes possible to establish yourself as an expert. When people begin to rate you highly in terms of your level of expertise, you become a credible source of the information they need.

Trust and respect also go along with credibility. Your visibility can also promote the credibility of your personal brand. The more people that know about your personal brand, the easier it is to accept that your brand is credible.

It Helps You Develop A Sense of Confidence

When you can share your strengths with others and get positive feedback, it helps in developing confidence in your abilities. As a personal brand, you will often have something unique to offer your target audience. This unique offering is what makes your personal brand unique.

As people begin to rely on you more, it emphasizes the unique strength of the personal brand – you. Through the confidence you gain, you can then start to identify other areas where you can better apply your strengths.

It Promotes Authenticity

The main quality of a successful personal brand is its authenticity and originality. The authenticity stems from the passion, values, skills, and goals of the personal brand. Through the personal brand, it is possible to become a relevant individual using just your skills.

To grow a personal brand, copying the brand voice of another individual or creating a persona that doesn't align with your real personality will not be effective. It is because most people on social media can quickly identify when a person is fake.

The personal brand requires individuals to focus on who they are and their unique skills to grow. It is how it promotes authenticity in individuals. By focusing on all your traits, it is possible to develop your weaknesses as an individual.

It Increases Your Value

A considerable benefit of a personal brand is the increase in value you can gain when you have a successful brand. This increase in value applies to the brand as well as any business you own. By increasing your online presence and gaining a significant amount of influence over your audience, a lot of companies will be looking to connect with your brand to attract your audience.

It Makes It Possible to Form Partnerships

Personal branding on social media allows you to get noticed with ease. The ability to find anyone online is a great tool that will work in your favor when you have a personal brand with a significant online presence. You will be able to find various companies, businesses, as well as other personal brands that will be willing to collaborate to increase their reach.

Recognition

The main feature of the Internet and social media is that it makes it possible to find anyone you want to connect with. Through a robust personal brand, it is a lot easier to locate you since your name becomes well known across various platforms. People don't have to go through any tedious processes when researching your brand and this helps improve the credibility of your brand.

Chapter 2:
The Future of Branding is Personal

Over the years, there have been various changes in the way people perform daily activities. A lot of these changes stemmed from advancements in technology. Due to the introduction of the Internet and email, it became easier for people to access and share information while the development of mobile phones made it possible for people to communicate with one another from anywhere and at any time.

Further development in how the Internet was being used led to the development of social media. Social media serves as a medium of communication between various individuals over the Internet. Popular social media platforms such as Twitter, Facebook, Instagram, and YouTube are what make it easy for people to communicate and share information over the Internet.

Development has also affected other areas of life including businesses, corporations, and brands. Previously, brands were associated with companies that had a massive influence over their customers. Most of the influence which these businesses had was as a result of advertising strategies which they implemented that made them popular among the population. The popularity of most brands was dependent on their ability to establish themselves as experts in the industry.

With the relative growth of the Internet in terms of ease of access and the development of social media platforms, it became possible for the ordinary user to develop a brand. The brand that an individual develops is what we refer to as a personal brand. Personal branding was steadily becoming an essential part of the daily life of an individual due to the impacts of social media. Defining a personal brand as the online reputation of an individual implies that everyone that has a social media account also has a personal brand they must manage.

So Why Then Is the Future of Branding Personal?

The shift from the traditional methods of advertising to social media marketing is one of the main reasons why the future of branding is personal. Unlike in previous years, when large companies and businesses had a major influence over the markets, it is now possible for one person to influence a large part of a market.

How Is This Possible?

Simple. Through a personal brand. A successful personal brand will usually have a massive number of followers that is more than what a lot of companies have on their social media channels. What this means is that as an individual, you can hold a lot more influence on others than any single corporate brand.

There are other reasons why you should consider the future of branding to be personal. Below are some of these reasons:

People Are Now Influenced by Who They Know, Like, And Trust

Unlike corporate brands, it is easy for an individual to connect with a personal brand. It is because they can interact with the individual running the personal brand. In a corporate brand, there is no one to whom customers can point to as the face of the brand. These brands sell their products and services to people by humanizing objects.

People are now looking to buy from individuals that have established themselves as experts within a niche. These individuals have influenced many through their personal brand. They are known by their audience, liked by them, and trusted explicitly.

Companies Are Looking Out for Individuals That Bring More Than Credentials to The Table

A lot of companies are moving towards hiring individuals that offer more than just the regular skill set. By considering the online presence of an individual, a company can identify those that can improve the value of the company by attracting new customers who will purchase their products.

Presently, a combination of hard skills, soft skills, and a significant online presence are some of the things that are necessary for getting a good job. These include the actual skills you need for the job, presentation skills, writing skills, leadership skills, organizational skills, and influence on the large social media platforms.

A Personal Brand Is A Tool That Will Promote Your Growth

If you build a successful personal brand, then you can use it in achieving any goal you set for yourself. Depending on how you use it, a personal brand can help in a fundraising campaign, moving from one career to the other, and growing a business from the early stages.

Chapter 3:
Designing a Purposeful Personal Brand

To design a purposeful brand, there are specific steps you need to take. These are steps that make it unique. A personal brand that is built with purpose will set the foundation for significant interaction with your audience and opportunities for growth.

The steps you need to take are straightforward and easy. Understanding the effect of each step is also vital to the growth of your brand.

Identify the Target Audience of Your Brand

Your target audience serves as the foundation of the personal brand. You can only grow a personal brand based on the target audience you choose. Selecting a target audience is your way of acknowledging that you cannot solve everyone's problems.

You have to define your ideal customer to be able to come up with a tagline and mission that will align with their expectations. The areas you should consider when selecting your target customer include:

- Gender

- Income

- Location

- Education level

- Age

You may also find other areas that can help you narrow down your target audience even more. It will be beneficial in ensuring that your content is meeting their needs and your ads are getting engagement.

Your Mission Statement

The mission statement of your brand is the reason why your personal brand is in existence. What do you intend to achieve through the personal brand? Your mission statement should be the passion that drives you to get up in the morning. Put this passion into a sentence that will be easily understood by your target audience.

As a definition of the purpose for the existence of the personal brand, a mission statement that your audience can relate to will help in gaining their trust. The statement is also essential in creating your strategy, logo, voice, personality, and tagline.

Analyzing Other Competing Brands

Research and analysis of other brands in a niche you select is crucial if you want to avoid replicating the same actions they have taken in the past. You want to make yourself aware of what other brands are doing but not to copy.

By performing your research, it becomes possible to differentiate your brand from the competition. A competitor spreadsheet can help in comparing the various actions from each competing brand within the niche. The information you should include in this spreadsheet are as follows:

- Quality of products and services they offer

- Online and offline marketing strategies

- Consistency in their branding across social media channels

- Feedback, reviews, and testimonials you can read to assess their performance

Benefits and Qualities That Customers Gain

For a brand to be successful, it has to offer certain attributes or benefits that others do not provide. These benefits or qualities do not depend on any form of budget. That is how a lot of smaller brands can compete with other larger brands.

When designing your personal brand, you must look inward to identify the unique benefits or qualities that your brand can offer its target audience. It is the reason that your target audience will have to select your personal brand in place of another brand.

The Brand Logo and Tagline

A brand logo and a tagline usually go together when developing your personal brand. These are often in the form of visuals that represent your brand. You may need to outsource the design of your brand logo to a professional to get the best look.

When anything that relates to your brand appears online, the logo and tagline should also be present. It is a visual representation of your brand that your customers will easily recognize.

Creating a great logo and tagline will require a substantial amount of time and money investment. The perception of the brand logo and tagline should be a visual identity that will align with your personal brand.

Create A Brand Voice

The niche you select, the brand mission, and the target audience all have a role in determining the brand voice you choose. The brand voice is the mode of communication you choose that will be the most effective in interacting with your audience. A brand voice can take any of the following forms:

- Authoritative

- Informative

- Professional

- Promotional

- Friendly

- Technical

- Service-oriented

- Conversational

Your ability to select the right brand voice will improve your chances of creating a great connection with your audience. Having a brand voice that is consistent across your various social media channels will make it easy for your audience to identify your brand anywhere they interact with it.

Chapter 4:
Social Media and Personal Branding

What Is Social Media?

Social media refers to all the Internet-based computer technology that promotes the creation of a community or virtual network. These networks or communities ease the process of sharing content that includes documents, photos, videos, and personal information among members.

Access to social media is possible through a web-based application or software that can be run on a smartphone, computer, or tablet. A lot of these applications are available for sending messages from one user to another. It is a vital feature of these applications as the initial development of social media was as a means of interaction between family and friends.

The growth of social media resulted in an expansion of its use. Nowadays, businesses incorporate the use of social media to reach and interact with their current and potential customers. The main strength of social media that makes it an invaluable asset to businesses is the ability to generate content to users around the world.

There are currently over 3 billion users who actively make use of social media platforms around the world, with each user having an average of 7.6 social media accounts (Smith, 2019).

Social media is based on Web 2.0 and features profiles and content that are generated by users. Several features are standard on all social media platforms, and they include the following:

User Account

A platform that allows users to sign up and create an account that will be personal to promote interaction is a social media platform. While there are still ways to interact with other users while remaining anonymous, there is still a need to create an account.

Newsfeed

A news feed offers real-live updates of the information that various users share on a social media platform. The information is the reason for connecting with multiple users in the first place.

Profile Page

This is where a user gives detailed information about themselves on the platform. The information that usually appears on the profile page includes the bio, photo, gender, recent activities, and more. It is a means of defining your personal brand.

Friends or Followers

Depending on the social media platform in use, the users you connect with on the platform will appear as friends or followers on your account. On some platforms, they are subscribers to your page.

Form of Engagement

The structure of engagement on most social media platforms is through likes and comments. There is a separate comment section where users can share their opinion on any content you post.

Customization

It won't feel like your account if you can't make specific changes to your account. Social media platforms allow users to edit specific settings on their pages that make it easy to use in a way that matches the user's preferences.

What Is Social Networking?

Social networking is the process of developing and nurturing relationships with other users on a social media platform. The network consists of friends, family, customers, colleagues, mentors, influencers, and so on. It is merely the online interaction between individuals who have interests that align.

Issues That Are Common with Social Media

Although social media remains a handy tool among its users, there are still certain issues that plague social media platforms. These issues go as far back as the initial launch of social media, and they have a lot of similarities with some of the problems with physical interaction. Below are some of the common issues:

Spam

Spamming involves a user, either a real individual or a bot, sending a lot of similar content to other users. These contents are often irrelevant to the user that receives them. In some cases, spamming may involve getting followed by a spambot.

Cyberstalking and Cyberbullying

Cyberbullying is simply the act of bullying that occurs online. Cyberstalking, on the other hand, involves a user getting the details of another online user and then stalking them physically. Social media promotes both issues since it provides the opportunity for users to interact the way they see fit and upload their personal details without restrictions.

Personal Image Manipulation

As a user on social media, most of the information you upload about yourself is often not a true reflection of your actual life. Users can decide to post only the best parts of their life while having the negative parts remain private.

The Spread of Fake News

Similar to rumors, social media also suffers from its fair share of fake news. Users can do anything they want on the platform, therefore, it's easy to find users that run phony news sites, promote their links, and generate massive traffic to the pages. Since everyone is reading without any research, it is easy to believe that the information on the site is accurate.

Overload of Information

A lot of social media users often have many friends or followers. If every one of these followers or friends decides to post content on the platforms, the information that will be available to a user will become too much that it is almost impossible to follow all of them.

Issues with Privacy or Security

Another significant problem with social media platforms is the privacy and safety of user information. Most platforms fall victims of hackers, and this results in access to information that users want to keep private.

Social Media and Personal Branding

Social media offers various platforms that are useful in growing a personal brand. Each of these platforms makes it easy to connect with other users and promotes interaction with these users. There are various reasons why it makes sense to develop a personal brand on each platform, and it is essential you understand each reason.

The advent of social media has made the process of building a personal brand a lot easier for individuals. Previously, only brands and individuals with money to invest in advertising and promotions could reach many individuals with ease. With the help of social media, it is now possible for an individual to connect to people from around the world directly from their home.

Depending on how an individual uses social media in developing a personal brand, they may gain an influence that will match that of a company. The opportunity for a single individual to attain this level of influence makes social media a potent tool in personal branding.

How Does Social Media Affect Your Personal Branding?

There are various ways through which social media can improve your personal branding. The following are some of the impacts that social media has on your personal branding:

Targeting Options

Social media offers users the opportunity to target a unique audience. By targeting the audience that will connect more with your brand, it is possible to increase traffic and grow the personal brand. An easy way to target an audience on social media is through ads, such as the easy to use Facebook ads.

Flexibility

Depending on where your target audience is most active, social media allows you to change your strategy to meet the needs of the audience. It is also possible to move from one platform to the other at no additional cost when building your personal brand on social media.

Access to Other Brands

Social media is a platform that is open to everyone. It includes both individuals and brands. As a personal brand, you can easily connect with other brands as well as your competition to assess their strategies and find voids that you can fill to boost your brand.

Analytics

The performance of your personal brand can be measured through the various tools available on social media platforms. Other software is also available to assess the engagement rate, reach, and growth of your personal brand on social media.

Innovation

Innovation on social media is visible in the development of new social media platforms and the incorporation of new features on already existing platforms. Features like live videos is an excellent way to promote interactions between your personal brand and your customers.

Mobile Friendly

Most social media platforms are accessible through mobile devices. This means your audience has access to your brand at anytime and anywhere.

Hashtags

The option to make use of hashtags on social media platforms makes it possible for you to improve the visibility of your brand. A hashtag is a form of unique keywords that a user can enter in a search entry to find accounts that have content that is relevant to a topic.

Unique Selling Proposition

Social media is a platform that has a lot of users and brands in the same industry or niche. If you have a personal brand in a niche, it is possible the services you will offer will be like other brands in the same niche.

To ensure you are different and make your brand stand out, you need to have a form of unique selling proposition. Through a unique selling proposition, you can reposition your brand in a way that is different from the other brands in the niche.

Your unique selling proposition should be the one thing that you do that is better or different from what others are doing. There are various areas where you can develop your unique selling proposition. It can be in your delivery speed, packaging, or customer relations.

Why Do You Need Your Personal Brand to Be Unique?

There are various reasons why a unique brand is essential for success. If you are not sure what these reasons are, below are some of the essential reasons for being unique when building a personal brand:

Your Brand Becomes Memorable

Being different in an industry is what makes your brand easy to remember. If your brand offers products or services that are similar to other brands in all aspects, there will be no way for your customers to differentiate your brand. The same applies to your personal brand.

Defining your personal brand based on who you are is one way to develop a unique personal brand. When your brand is unique, it becomes authentic, original, and memorable.

Your Customers Will Appreciate the Brand

If you can offer your audience something different from what they find regularly, they will flock to your brand. As humans, we appreciate things that break away from the norm. The burst of freshness it provides is what keeps us going.

If your brand can make a positive difference, it will become popular in the niche. It is the value of being unique.

The Value of Your Brand Increases

When you decide to reject the things that people take as normal and positively revolutionize their views, you are being unique. Only a few personal brands are willing to go to this extent. If you are ready to take the risk and provide a positive kind of revolution, the value of your brand will increase.

It is merely your target audience showing that they are tired of getting the same old things in a repackaged form. People don't want to interact with a brand that follows the same process of the masses.

Developing A Unique Brand

There are simple methods you can implement when building a personal brand to make it unique. Below are some of these methods.

Identify and Focus on Your Strengths

To create a unique brand, you first have to come up with the strengths that are peculiar to the brand. Your personal brand is built around you as an individual, so this step will require an inward look at yourself.

Your goal is to discover an ability, talent, skill, or approach to solving specific problems that only you can offer. Some resources that can help in identifying your unique strengths include an Enneagram test or Myers-Briggs Type Indicator test.

If you focus on these strengths, you can gain positive progress and fulfillment. It is vital you stop focusing on your weaknesses to avoid letting self-doubt creep in.

Connect with People That Inspire You

There are lots of people who may inspire you through their approach in life, work ethics, or any other way. These individuals may be doing better than you and are currently at the top of their field. Now is not the time to compare yourself to these individuals, you should focus more on learning from them.

You can reach out and connect with these individuals to learn more from them. How did they overcome specific struggles? How did they discover their strengths? What did they do about their weaknesses?

You can learn a lot from interaction with others. Connecting with your competitors within a niche can also be a step in the right direction. There may be pointers that they can give you due to their experience in the niche.

Learn from Failure

Developing a unique brand may not occur on your first try. You may start building a personal brand and fail due to some bad choices along the line. Learning from these failures can help you grow as a person.

Failure provides an opportunity for you to revise your personal branding strategy, reassess your goals, and then start over from the beginning. It will also help you understand that in some cases, no matter the level of planning, things don't always go your way.

There are lots of prominent individuals that failed multiple times in their journey to success. Don't accept failure as the end.

Form Partnerships with Others

When creating a personal brand, a partner may be all you need to make your way to success. A partner is someone that will remain calm when you are losing yourself so that they can guide you back on the right path.

A wife, friend, family, or colleague, anyone can be your partner. A partner will also be able to offer a unique perspective on anything you decide to incorporate when building your personal brand. These are some of the values that you gain from this individual.

Chapter 5:
Creating a Personal Brand on YouTube

What Is YouTube?

YouTube is a website and social media platform that supports the hosting of videos that users upload. These videos are available for others to view and comment on as a form of engagement.

Content in Video Format Is More Effective in Establishing Yourself as An Expert

In developing your personal brand, there are a lot of things you will want to showcase to your target audience. This includes the knowledge you have gained from reading and through personal experience. Putting thoughts into words may sometimes be very difficult to achieve.

Creating content in a video format also makes it possible to be more expressive in your thoughts. In case you already have excellent writing skills, using a video format can be a great way to show your audience that you have a lot more to offer. This includes your ability to make presentations and unique facial expressions that make it easy to connect with your audience.

You Become Easily Noticeable to Your Target Audience

When creating a personal brand, your main aim is to become easy to find, identify, and reach by your target audience. By growing your personal brand on YouTube, you are also promoting yourself on a platform that ranks second in terms of size after the Google search engine (Marion, 2018).

It Helps in Making Your Brand Stand Out

Through YouTube, you can create a personal brand that will be unique in comparison to others within your niche. To achieve this, all you need to do is create video content that is compelling and valuable to your target audience while showcasing the personality of your personal brand in the video.

To make yourself unique, you must differentiate yourself in the presentation of your content. This is where videos become very important. You can showcase your creativity in each video, and by bringing in your unique personality, it becomes possible for your viewers to identify your brand.

Most Individuals Enjoy Video Content

From the growth of YouTube as a video sharing platform, there are a few things everyone can learn. One of the most critical lessons is the fact that a lot of people love to view videos and share these videos.

If this is the case, taking advantage of the YouTube platform means you can promote your content to your target audience, and if it offers value, they will be willing to share with other users.

Niche Selection for Your Personal Brand on YouTube

Creating the right video content for your audience requires you to know the target audience of your personal brand. Identifying the target audience becomes easier when you select a niche.

Niche selection is essential if you hope to monetize your YouTube channel through affiliate marketing in the future. To ensure that there is an intent and purpose behind every video you upload on your YouTube channel, you need to have a niche.

What Is A Niche?

A niche is a small part of a more significant industry. It is a section with preferences and needs that may often differ from the more significant industry. Separating a larger market or industry into a niche makes it easier to meet the needs and demands of the market.

Deciding on The Best YouTube Niche

Most people usually open a YouTube channel with a niche in mind. It is often the case for individuals with particular skills and knowledge that make them stand out. These skills are usually teachable, and that makes them well sought after by many viewers. An example of some skills that can make a great niche on YouTube includes AutoCAD skills, video editing skills, photography skills, and more.

Nonetheless, starting a YouTube channel without any skill is also possible. All you need to do is to perform an assessment to determine the best niche that will suit your personality.

Below are some of the things you should consider and assess when selecting a niche:

Passion

The topic of any niche you choose should be something that you are very passionate about. It should interest and fascinate you every time you decide to talk about it to anyone. It also implies that you have in-depth knowledge regarding the niche.

There are numerous reasons why you should be passionate about any niche you select. First, creating the content of your channel will be up to you. You need to generate new ideas to discuss in your videos. If you don't have the passion for the niche, you will end up in frustration and anger when it becomes too difficult to come up with a topic.

Another reason why passion is essential is to enable you to connect easily with your viewers. When you create a video on a topic you are passionate about, your viewers can notice the enthusiasm in your voice, and they know that your passion is genuine.

Demand

The growth of your channel depends on the level of engagement from your viewers. If you are not getting enough viewers on the channel, there is no chance of the channel growing.

Before selecting any niche, it is vital you check for the demand. Are there users searching for keywords relating to the niche? It is an important question you need to answer before selecting a niche for your brand.

In the case of an individual that is opening a YouTube channel to share a lifehack or a hobby, the demand may not matter at all. In the case of a personal brand, if there is no audience to view the videos, then it is all for nothing.

To ensure that the niche is in demand, different tools are available to help in getting the necessary information. You can use both Google Trends and Google AdWords Keyword Planner.

Google Trends is an excellent tool to use in identifying how much users engage with a topic. Is the engagement changing with time? Or is it seasonal? A popular example of a seasonal topic is Christmas.

The Google AdWords Keyword Planner is a tool that can help you assess the performance of a keyword on the Internet. By inputting a keyword, you can view the number of searches the keyword has gotten in a month. Simply create an account and include all these keywords to see all the information you need, including the level of competition.

Competition

The level of competition you should expect depends on the number of active YouTubers present in any niche you select. If a niche has a high number of active YouTubers, it means it is oversaturated. Getting your channel to stand out in a niche that is oversaturated will be very difficult.

You can select a niche that is undersaturated if you don't have any niche in mind when deciding to build a personal brand on YouTube. If you have the option of being flexible with your decision, you can choose a niche that has low competition but high demand.

On the other hand, if you are expanding into YouTube to promote your content or product, then you don't have the option of changing your niche. If you end up in a niche that is oversaturated, all you need to do is develop a new strategy. You can have a strategy in which you make use of keywords that have little competition and steadily work your way up to the more competitive keywords.

Learn from Other YouTube Channels

There are various things you can learn from others on YouTube. You can learn a lot if you are monitoring other channels that are in a similar niche. The information you need will be available if you take the time to watch some of their videos and read some of the comments their viewers have posted.

Some of the vital information you can gain from other YouTube channels includes the following:

- The type of content to post

- How they promote engagement

- What the feedback from viewers is like

- How you can improve on what they offer

- Why they have a lot of viewers

This process is a form of research that helps you identify areas that are currently being overlooked in the niche and cover these areas. Nonetheless, you can also cover topics that other channels have already discussed. What you have to do with yours is to make sure it is authentic and has a unique approach.

You can outperform your competition by bringing in transparency to a niche or engaging in paid advertising and promotion. There are other benefits of a high level of competition in a niche. It usually implies that the niche you have selected will be profitable in the long run.

When dealing with a high level of competition in a niche, always remember, quality is better than quantity. High-quality content will make you stand out from the crowd.

There are specific niches that are very popular on YouTube. If you decide to venture into any of these niches, you must be ready to go the extra mile to make your channel successful. Some of these niches include:

- Tutorials

- Fashion

- Gaming

- Travel

- Food

- Product reviews

- How To videos

- Vlogs

- Tech videos

- Animals

- Humor

- Beauty

How Focused Should Your Niche Be?

Selecting a niche for your YouTube channel is a positive step towards the success of the channel. Nonetheless, you need to be sure that the focus of the niche is not so narrow that it becomes an issue.

A niche that is too narrow is one in which you are going to run out of topics to discuss very soon. It is a kind of niche that you want to avoid as it can ruin your channel. When selecting the niche, make sure there are continuous product releases, news updates, and activity within the niche.

If there are a lot of people that are passionate about the niche, then it will be easy to find something to talk about. A good niche should be able to stand the test of time.

You should aim for a niche with a reasonable number of individuals actively purchasing products within the niche. Active consumers usually promote engagement within a niche. These are the people that need the product reviews, tutorials, and how-to videos you offer. The purchases also have to be spread across various products.

Strategies for Success on YouTube

There are various strategies you can implement for your channel to be successful on YouTube. Combining these strategies will have a huge impact on the growth of your channel. Some strategies you should implement are as follows:

Identify and Use Keywords That Are Relevant to Your Niche

Once you have chosen a niche for your channel, the next step is to start building your personal brand around this niche. Like the Google search engine, YouTube also ranks the results it provides when viewers use the search entry. For any niche you select, it is crucial you find a keyword that a lot of viewers search for on the platform.

There are various tools available to achieve the results you desire. One such tool is the External Keyword Tool that Google offers. By using this tool, it is possible to identify the competitiveness of a keyword, other related keywords, and most importantly, the search volumes for the keyword.

Any keyword you select should be one with a search volume of at least 1,000, so you can grow your personal brand and your YouTube channel. Since you are still building your brand, a keyword with relatively low competitiveness can be very helpful.

Do Your Research

Regardless of the niche you choose, it is possible there is already content related to a topic you want to discuss. Performing extensive research will reveal the channels with similar content. Once you identify these channels, you need to take time to go through the videos they have and identify areas that they may have missed.

You can also make your presentation in a unique way that will differentiate it from the other videos available. If your niche is profitable, then it will be competitive.

Have an Objective

Your passion for a niche or topic can cause you to derail from the main point when making a YouTube video. To avoid such mistakes, it is crucial you state a clear objective for any video you create.

By following an objective, it becomes easier to focus on what you intend to deliver to your target audience. An objective can also be beneficial in creating a clear definition of your niche. If you are thinking of creating a YouTube channel for Do-It-Yourself (DIY) tutorials, your objective can help in narrowing down the niche of the channel to DIYs.

Problem-Solving Is Crucial

Any niche you select will have a target audience that you want to reach out to. The only reason why the target audience will keep viewing your videos is that it offers value to them. The value you provide to these viewers is often a way to solve a problem they are facing.

Solving the problems of the viewers may be in the form of tutorial videos, product reviews, or recommending the best product for a task. To determine the type of problems your target audience are facing, you can use any of the methods below:

- Go through niche forums

- Interact with members of the target audience in one-on-one conversations

- Examine the popular keywords that members of the audience input in the search entry

High-Quality Content Reformatting

In your goal of building a personal brand on YouTube, you may have started the same process on a different social media platform. If this is the case, then the growth of the personal brand on that platform is often a result of the high-quality content you offer users on that platform.

If you have any content that is of high-quality in any other format, then it is time to convert it into a video format. You may have a guide on how to use a particular product on your blog but making this content into a video will make things a lot easier for your audience. People love simplicity.

There are occasions when you must create content from scratch. At other times, it is essential you reformat your existing content to meet the demands of your audience. Any content you are reformatting must be content that has a high engagement rate on your other social media channels.

Brand Your Channel

Although it is a personal brand, you still want it to look as professional as possible. By branding your YouTube channel, you are attributing a certain kind of appearance or theme to the channel. It is an appearance that your audience will quickly notice anytime they view your content.

Proper branding will increase your chances of getting viewers to subscribe to the channel. Branding may appear in the form of visual branding, such as the logo you put on your videos, the transition affects you use, and so on. It's what makes your brand stand out. Other forms of branding you can use on a video include the addition of a short and interesting piece about yourself and a custom URL on your channel header.

Remember to Promote Your Videos

In addition to the viewers you want to reach on the YouTube platform, you also want to attract users from other social media platforms. To attract these users, it is essential you promote content from your channel to these users.

Promoting content on other social media platforms is known as cross-promotion. You can promote your YouTube videos on any channel including Facebook, Instagram, Twitter, LinkedIn, and Pinterest. On Facebook, you can take advantage of the option to post a teaser video. Anyone who views the teaser video and likes it can follow a link to your YouTube channel to see the full video.

By posting teaser videos on platforms that support it, you can promote engagement across your social media channels.

Consistency Is Vital - Upload Content Frequently

Creating a high-quality video usually takes a lot of time and effort. It is crucial you don't compromise on either of these when building your personal brand. Nonetheless, it is vital you limit the time you spend on creating a video to a single week.

To ensure the growth of your YouTube channel, you need to post at least one video every week. It is a consistent activity that will yield a lot of benefits for your personal brand.

To promote consistency, you need to create a schedule that you will follow. Through this schedule, you will be able to post content at the same time every week. Once you are consistent with the day and time of your release, your audience will also be able to follow the schedule you have set up for the channel.

Consistency also covers the type of content you post on your channel. The content you post should relate to the niche you have selected. It should follow the objectives you have set for the personal brand or else you will slowly lose your subscribers.

Deliver Your Message in A Short Time

Most viewers love a very short video. No matter how much people love your brand, they won't sit through a 30-minute video for an explanation that can be done in 5 minutes.

It is best you get straight to the point. This is vital when creating how-to videos or any form of tutorial video. The opportunity to watch you act already gives them an advantage, so you don't need to bore users with overly lengthy stories.

If it is necessary that you give an elaborate explanation on the same topic, you can make another video to solve the issue.

Using Paid Promotion

Getting your content to your target audience may often require a little money investment. On YouTube, you can take advantage of the paid promotion in the form of "Featured Videos."

This feature is an excellent form of promotion that will get your videos across to a lot of viewers in a very short time. It is a simple process of improving the reach of a video. If you decide to utilize the paid promotion feature, you should be sure the video is of excellent quality. High-quality videos usually yield better results.

Engage with Active Users on The Platform

Sometimes, it is crucial you interact with specific users that are very active on the YouTube platform. These are users that people are familiar with because they are continually offering value to other users on the platform.

By getting your content to the notice of these users, you can benefit more from the comments they make on your videos. Comments usually promote engagement on the content.

Create Your Videos in The Form of a Series

As discussed earlier, most viewers want a video that is short and straight to the point. So, what happens when you have a lot of information on a specific topic?

The simple solution is to create a series for your viewers. These are multiple videos focusing on the same topic. You can put these videos into a playlist to allow the users to transition from one video to the next without doing anything.

To fully understand this process, you can liken it to binge-watching your favorite series on Netflix. On YouTube, the next video is included in the Up Next section automatically. The feature only works if a user turns on the autopay function.

The Creator Studio makes it possible for you to update a playlist to a series playlist. The first step is to open the Playlists menu from the Video manager tab. You then locate the playlist you want to change and click on the edit button. Open the Playlist settings on the edit screen to pick the "Set as Official Series for This Playlist" option.

Unlike the regular playlists, you can place a video in only one series playlist. To make the most of the option available to you, use only your best videos when creating a series playlist.

Your Personality Is Your Authenticity

Success on YouTube depends on how well you can connect with your target audience. It also has a significant impact in making you stand out from your competition. To be successful, you must avoid copying any other YouTuber.

To grow your personal brand in a niche, you have to offer a unique angle. How you present your videos, your voice, and your expressions all add to the appeal of your video.

Your Videos Should Include Links

When you decide to add links to your videos, you need these links to redirect users to other high-quality videos you have to offer or to your blog. To insert links, you can make use of annotations. Nonetheless, you should be careful about how you implement these annotations. Your priority is for users to have a great experience watching your videos.

There are other navigation features you can include in your videos to help users explore your channel. These include a featured video overlay and a branding watermark.

Get Viewers to Subscribe

Subscriptions to your YouTube channel is one way to know that your channel is experiencing growth. When a viewer subscribes to your channel, they can learn about any new video you post on your channel.

In each video you post on your YouTube channel, you should remind users to subscribe to your channel. An increase in subscriptions also implies that more viewers are engaging with your content. You can also ask viewers to comment on a video to promote engagement on your YouTube channel.

Growing your subscribers' list doesn't require any form of payment. YouTube also allows you to view your list of subscribers. If you must pay for people to subscribe to your channel, you won't get the engagement you desire. Other YouTube viewers will also lose their trust in your brand and the channel as soon as they discover what you have been up to.

As simple as it may sound, simply asking your viewers to subscribe can yield a lot of positive results for your channel.

Use High-Quality Thumbnails

Thumbnails often have a significant impact on the growth of your channel. The thumbnail of a video is the still image that appears when your video has been searched for on YouTube. Depending on how catchy your thumbnail appears to viewers, it can increase the number of views that your video receives.

You can decide to import a custom image to use on a video. There is no harm in using a custom image. Remember, users will scan through the search results to find a video to watch. A thumbnail that gets their attention is very valuable. It doesn't matter how much value your content offers, if your thumbnail can't get users to click on it, then you won't be getting as many views as you may want.

Use YouTube Analytics

On your YouTube channel, there is an analytics section available to help improve the performance of your channel. You can quickly assess the performance of the channel through the available metrics. You can also use it to compare the performance of various videos on your channel and determine why one video outperforms another.

Success Strategies on YouTube - Mistakes You Should Avoid

Growing your personal brand on YouTube requires a lot of action on your part. These actions have a direct impact on the performance of the channel.

Similarly, there are also certain actions you need to avoid if you intend to remain successful on the platform. Here, you can learn about some of the common mistakes that can ruin a YouTube channel.

Copying Metadata from Other Youtubers

A trend you may notice on several new YouTube channels is that they don't take time to create unique metadata for their videos. They simply copy the metadata of an already existing YouTube channel. In most cases, the videos they copy are usually those that have been very successful on the platform.

While this may seem like a good idea, it paints a bad picture for you as an individual and your personal brand. The YouTuber you copied may end up blacklisting you, and you may lose any opportunity you had to connect with them.

Not Collaborating with Other Youtubers
When you decide to build a personal brand, it is often because you have something to share or a skill to promote. Developing a single skill helps you stand out in a niche. Your channel will be built around the skill you intend to promote.

On YouTube, it is easy to reach the subscribers of another YouTube channel. All you need to do is to collaborate with the said YouTuber. Look for a popular YouTuber within your niche that has a lot of viewers but doesn't offer the skills you have developed.

If you have developed a skill in graphics or logo designing, you can reach out to the YouTuber and offer to create a design for them. You can then ask for a mention in their upcoming video. It is how you can have the YouTube community help grow your brand.

Losing Your Originality
Originality can also refer to your authenticity or personality. If your videos don't have a unique pattern, then your videos don't have a

personality. In building your personal brand, you should avoid creating videos that are similar to the current trends on the platform.

By making originality a priority, you can create videos that are unique and which will sell you to your potential viewers.

Forgetting the Call-To-Action (CTA) Features on YouTube

Cross-promotion is an essential aspect of building a personal brand you must not forget. You can use the CTA features on YouTube to redirect users to your Facebook or Twitter account. Merely adding a hyperlink to the description box is all you need.

Hyperlinks are beneficial because people prefer to avoid doing anything that requires too much effort. The hyperlink allows users to click on it and it will go directly to the page they desire.

Straying Away from Your Brand's Focus

When you are looking to get more views and subscribers on your YouTube channel, it is easy to opt for content that you know is trending on the platform. It is crucial you understand that building a personal brand will take time. Patience is one of the essential qualities you need to see things through to the end.

You need to be consistent in your approach and have a long-term strategy in place.

Overlooking Content from Other Youtubers

Your passion for a niche may not be enough to inspire your next great idea. Watching videos from different Youtubers within your niche and other influencers can provide the lucky break you need.

Once you get your inspiration, remember to remain authentic, use a voice that is unique to your brand, and produce valuable content that is short and straight to the point. These are just some of the essentials for success on YouTube.

Forgetting About Your Subscribe Button

If you are running a YouTube channel and you don't remember that there is a subscribe button for your users to make use of, then you will lose out on a lot of opportunities for growth. Always remember to mention the subscribe button in your videos to promote the growth of the channel.

The first week of running a YouTube channel and the first video you post is not going to bring instant success for your personal brand. Learning to make use of the various strategies available, tips, and being patient will surely get you to the goal you desire.

Chapter 6:
Creating a Personal Brand on Facebook

What Is Facebook?

Facebook is a platform that allows users to interact by posting content. The content that users can post on this social networking site includes images, videos, texts, and links. Depending on the preference of the users, content can be open to the public or just a select group of users, such as family and friends.

Facebook was launched in 2004 and was created by Mark Zuckerberg and Eduardo Saverin who were both students at Harvard University at the time (Nations, 2019).

As a social networking platform, Facebook is available to anyone around the world and has some excellent features that are designed to meet the needs of businesses and brands. The beauty of Facebook as a social network is in the opportunity it offers its users to keep in touch with family, friends, colleagues, and reconnect with past acquaintances.

Another key feature of Facebook is that it is child-friendly in the sense that it doesn't support users posting adult content. To show how much the platform detests such content, any user that is reported is banned from the platform. In terms of privacy, users can customize their profile to avoid exposing their information to the entire world.

Benefits of Facebook

To both your personal brand and for personal use, Facebook offers a number of benefits that are very valuable. Below are some of the benefits you can enjoy on the platform:

- It allows users to stream live videos which is a feature you need if you want to interact with your audience in real-time.

- The privacy settings make it possible for you to restrict the type of content that will appear on your Facebook account in case it might hurt your personal brand.

- It promotes engagement by offering users the option of liking, commenting, and sharing content and posts that gets their attention.

- It provides a form of paid advertising that enables your brand to reach your target audience with ease.

- You have the option of opening a fan page, business page, Facebook group, or all three to promote your brand.

Getting Started with The Facebook Platform

Facebook is easy to use and getting started should be stress-free. All you need to do is sign up on the platform, and then you can move on to the process of setting up your Facebook account.

Creating A Detailed Facebook Profile

Signing up and creating a Facebook account is free to anyone that desires. In achieving your goal of building a personal brand, it is necessary you create a Facebook profile that is easily accessible and identifiable by your potential followers and customers.

There are four areas of your Facebook profile that you need to populate with information if you intend to reach your target audience with ease. These are:

- A visible name on your Facebook profile

- Custom URL/username

- Profile picture

- Timeline cover photo

Optimizing these four areas of your Facebook profile is crucial if you want to reach the right target audience. Here is a brief look at what each area covers:

A Visible Name on Your Facebook Profile

Since everything you will be doing on the platform is to promote your personal brand, you need to select a name that will be easily identifiable. This name will appear at the top of your Facebook profile.

Depending on how you intend to develop your brand, you may use your real name or another name that better represents your personal brand. A name that better represents your brand should be a name that you already use on other social platforms.

It is not the time to be coming up with a new nickname just because you think it is catchy. You want your audience from other channels like Twitter and Instagram to find you easily.

Custom URL/Username

The option of a username is an essential part of the Facebook platform. Facebook is a platform with over 2 billion unique users that log on to the platform every month (Cooper, 2018). This means that getting the name you want may be very difficult.

To solve this problem, you can create a custom username/URL for your Facebook profile. You can include this URL on your email signature or add it to your business card. You may also know this URL as the vanity URL.

Profile Picture

The profile picture is another area of your Facebook profile that must be made public. As a personal brand, you need to choose a profile picture carefully. You want your profile picture to send an excellent message to your target audience.

For a personal brand, the profile picture should be a professional picture of yourself. It is also essential that the picture is the same across all your social media platforms.

Timeline Cover Photo

The cover photo is a header image that appears on the timeline of a Facebook user. It is 851 x 315 dpi, and it is useful for promoting your brand logo. It is an image that is also made public, so it should be used wisely.

Adding Other Details

In addition to the four areas discussed above, there are other areas that you need to populate with information to optimize your Facebook profile. Some of the details you can include on Facebook include the following:

- Educational experience

- Work experience

- Social channel links

These additional details provide an avenue for you to give information on who you are, what you do, your background, and more. This is critical information that can help you better connect with your target audience.

With a personal brand, building a network is vital for growth. The inclusion of a field for users to fill in their education information makes it possible to connect with former classmates. Adding your work experience can also connect you with other users in the same industry.

The links option enables you to include links to other social media platforms such as Twitter, LinkedIn, YouTube, Instagram, your blog or website, and more. It is an excellent form of cross-promotion for your personal brand.

Ensuring you fill in all the necessary details will improve the ranking of your Facebook profile or page on a search engine. It will also help improve your traffic.

Building A Personal Brand on Facebook

Like on other platforms, there are certain steps you can take to grow your personal brand on Facebook. Understanding and implementing each step will help you grow your brand correctly.

Create A Strategy for Personal Branding

Achieving success in personal branding requires a strategy that you must consistently follow. The strategy you develop should be dependent on your passion, your personality, and your goals. The target audience will also significantly influence the branding strategy you follow.

Creating a personal branding strategy is the first step you need to take before creating a Facebook account. Developing a strategy first gives you full control of how you want to create the personal brand right from the early stages of the account. If you need to use an already existing account to create the personal brand, you will need to make some changes that may turn out to be quite tricky.

Your branding strategy should cover everything about the platform and how you intend to use the platform in growing your personal brand. This includes the content you will post, the type of media that will be available, the links you post, the topics you discuss, and more. The branding strategy should be developed in a way that it can help build the reputation of your personal brand positively.

Include Excellent Visuals

An excellent feature of Facebook is the option of combining your images with texts. In truth, a lot of people may miss your post if there is no visual to go along with the post. To ensure you are getting through to your target audience, you should try creating a visual for any text content you are posting.

A quick look at various Facebook statistics shows that users engage more with photos and video content (Moeller, 2019). As a personal brand, your goal is to get your target audience to engage with your page. Engagement on your page will also help in growing your reach on the platform.

By looking at the various popular social media platforms, it is easy to notice that a lot of people love platforms that offer the opportunity for users to share both images and videos in addition to any text-based content they post. Learning to take advantage of this trend is an effective strategy to grow your personal brand from scratch.

There are different ways of creating visuals on Facebook. Depending on your skill level, you may decide to use Photoshop in creating your visuals. Another common tool available is Canva. These tools make it possible for you as the user to create high-quality visuals that can promote engagement with friends, followers, and potential customers.

Go for High-Quality and Not Large Quantity
Reach on Facebook depends mostly on the quality of a post rather than the quantity of posts you can upload within a short time. A high-quality post is one that has a lot of engagement from friends, fans, and followers.

In building your personal brand, you need to upload more high-quality content to increase your reach on the platform. High-Quality content with a high engagement rate implies that there are a lot of users commenting, liking, or sharing the post. A post that gets a high engagement rate is sure to reach a more significant number of Facebook users.

It is also essential you are redirecting traffic to your other platforms like your website or blog through high-quality content. Content that causes people to pick sides or that is nostalgic is sure to promote engagement. As a personal brand, it is often best to avoid controversial posts.

Let Your Text-Based Posts and Videos Be Short

A picture is worth a thousand words. It is a saying that holds true even on social media. It might as well be the reason why images get more engagement than text-based posts. Besides, a glance is usually all it takes for a user to get the hidden message behind an image.

The vital information you should take from the explanation above is the time frame. Users want content they can read and understand within a very short time. To ensure you get the best engagement on your text-based posts, you should aim for content that doesn't exceed 50 characters (Moeller, 2019).

Just because Facebook allows it doesn't mean it is the best for building your brand. Although you can upload videos of up to 240 minutes, posting a video no more than 4 minutes is recommended for getting the best engagement from Facebook users (Moeller, 2019).

The way each platform works is often different, so it is essential you learn to adapt. Learning to pass your message across in just 50 characters can be very difficult if you are well-versed in curating SEO-compliant content. Nonetheless, you must provide what your audience requires.

Update Your Facebook Privacy Settings

Although some of the information on the profile must be available to the public, there is other information that may not. It is up to you to decide who can see this information.

This includes your photos, comments, updates, and other information. In building your personal brand on Facebook, the first step is for you to decide what information is suitable for you to post.

If you have some of your close friends on your Facebook profile, they may decide to post and tag you in some personal pictures that your audience may not like. In this case, you may choose to block users from tagging your account directly in any post. It makes it difficult for people to link a post to you as an individual on the platform.

In Facebook's privacy settings, you can make your account visible to all users on Facebook or limit which parts of your account users can view. A fully public account will have a wider reach, so it is vital you make it friendly to anyone visiting.

Create A Facebook Group

There are limitations in your reach when you are running a Facebook profile. Instead, you should create a Facebook group to grow a community for your personal brand. To promote the growth of the group, it is essential you find a way to promote it to your audience. You can do this by sharing a link for users to join on other channels like your website, blog, and so on. Creating a Facebook ad can also help and you can reduce the number of ads once the group attracts a large number of members.

The beauty of a group is the opportunity to have ongoing discussions. Other benefits include the reduction in the cost of marketing, the opportunity to promote your channels and products, as well as the continuous growth of your audience.

Creating a group is often very easy, but that doesn't mean it will be successful. There are various steps you can take to ensure the success of any group you decide to create for your personal brand.

The first step in creating a group that is sure to be successful is to invite active individuals. Any Facebook user that is active will surely love to engage and interact with other users. Engagement and interaction are two qualities you need from any member in your group.

These individuals should be people that you know. No one wants to join a group without any content so these users will help grow the content during the early stages of the group. It helps define your group as fun and interactive to your target audience.

The next step is to decide on the discussions in the group. You may choose to pick controversial topics for a group discussion as these are sure to boost engagement. Case studies can also help in promoting discussion among members.

Another step you should consider is deciding if you should create a support group for your audience. If you are building a personal brand in the finance industry or fitness industry, a support group is usually necessary.

Running A Facebook Page

Although it is still the same platform, Facebook provides the opportunity for users to create a profile, group, and page. The different features you get from each of these options makes it necessary to open an account for your personal branding strategy. An artist, band, or public figure Facebook page is the most suitable.

A Facebook page is unique in the sense that it is created for businesses, organizations, brands, celebrities, and bands. In your case, you are building a brand, and if you play your cards right, you will also turn out a celebrity. Unlike the Facebook profile, you are going to be getting "fans" on your page. These are Facebook users that like your page and there is no limit to the number of fans you can have on the page.

The page also operates like a Facebook profile, so it is easy to get a handle on it. Nonetheless, a unique feature that makes a Facebook page stand out is the Facebook Insights tool. Using the Insights tool, it is possible to analyze some critical Facebook metrics and assess the performance of your personal brand on the platform.

Making Use of Facebook Insights

The Insights menu is available on the top navigation menu of the Facebook Page. Clicking on it takes you to the Insights dashboard.

There are various sections of the Insights dashboard, and each offers a unique analysis of your page. Learning to use each part in your analysis is vital in getting a clear picture of your performance.

The Overview section looks at all the important activities that took place on the page. These activities are those within the last week, and it includes the page likes, engagement, and post reach.

The like section shows the number of users that have liked the page in the past seven days, and it includes the net likes, total likes, and where the likes came from. It is an excellent tab for assessing the growth of the brand's page.

The post reach offers information on the number of Facebook users that viewed any of the content from the page. It includes other metrics such as the total reach, likes, unlike, and so on.

There is also a visits section that identifies the number of users that are visiting the page. Also, it also gives you access to the location of these users. It is subdivided into the page and tab visits, and the external referrers. The page and tab visits show the number of times other users viewed the page or the tabs within the page, while the external referrers indicate the number of users that visited the Facebook page using a link from another website. These websites may sometimes be known while others may be unknown.

The post section is vital in determining the type of content that your target audience finds enjoyable. The metrics that are available in this section include the post type, the time when fans are online, and the top posts from pages you are watching.

In the video section, you will find video views, top videos, and 30-second views. The top videos are those that have the highest number of viewers that watched for at least three seconds. The 30-second view shows the number of users that watched the video for at least the first 30 seconds.

In the people section, you can assess some key metrics like the number of people engaged, reached, and fans. These are essential metrics to help learn more about your audience. The fans metrics will indicate the age, language, location, and gender of the users liking your page.

Keep Expanding Your Network

The only sure way to grow your personal brand is to keep increasing the number of users that learn about your brand, become friends with the brand, and follow the brand. To achieve this, you must also think about what you can do outside the Facebook platform.

To expand your network, one step you can take is to build an email list. If you already have one, you should look to add more people to the list. As the list keeps growing, it is vital you import these new contacts into your Facebook account. You can also redirect users through your website, blog, or other social media channels.

Post Regular Status Updates

Regularly updating your status is another easy way to show that you are active on the platform. In addition, a single update will also reach your target audience without any extra work on your part.

Creating an exceptional status that will captivate your audience is essential. Any status update on the platform should follow your personal branding strategy to make it very useful. You may use the status update to promote a new blog article, inform your audience of a new project, or mention a new interest. The goal is to ensure that your audience knows what you are up to and learn about your opinions on specific topics or events.

Have A Clearly Defined Audience

A clearly defined target audience is an essential aspect of building a successful personal brand on Facebook. If you have a well-defined audience, it means you understand the needs and expectations of the audience as well as the type of content they interact with regularly.

The main reason why you may struggle to grow your personal brand is if the content you are providing doesn't align with the interests of your target audience.

To connect with your audience, you need to know your audience. There are bits of information that can help you learn more about your target audience. These include the gender, income level, education level, occupation, location, language, and age. Learning all these bits of information about your target audience makes it possible to connect with them on a more personal level.

If you know that most of the members of your target audience are in their early twenties, then you can easily promote engagement by sharing content that is applicable to them at this age. The information you share may cover issues such as investing or building a side hustle.

Provide A Captivating Headline

A lot of users will want to read a post if the headline is appealing. When posting a link on your profile or group, you need to come up with a catchy headline that will get your audience to click on the link. If you post a link with a random headline, it may generate a minimal engagement rate.

The headline you come up with should be directed at your target audience. This headline is not the same as the link description so ensure you make the most of this additional field.

Use Facebook Ads

Facebook ads are an easy way to promote content and generate more leads on the platform. These ads offer a form of paid reach, and the number of users that get to see your content through paid reach is often very reasonable. Also, it takes a shorter time in comparison to organic reach.

Using Facebook ads is quite easy. All you need to do is open the Facebook Ads Manager and create an ad campaign. You can then choose an objective for the campaign, and this can be an awareness, consideration, or conversion objective. The next step is to set your target audience and budget for the campaign. You can then create your advertisement and choose an ad placement before placing an order.

You should understand that placing an ad on Facebook is at a cost but in the end, it is usually worth the money spent.

Chapter 7:
Creating a Personal Brand on Twitter

What Is Twitter?

Twitter is a social media platform that enables communication between members of the community through tweets. A tweet is a message you send on the Twitter platform. A tweet is often a random message or thought that you post with the hope that other users will find meaning in the tweet.

Microblogging is an alternative description of Twitter that is becoming very popular. The use of Twitter helps users to discover people with similar interests, companies, and brands.

Twitter as a social media platform is straightforward to use and allows users to connect with ease. It also enables users to go through the tweets of other users by simply scrolling through the Twitter feed. Since each tweet has a limited number of characters, it is effortless to go through a large number of the tweets on a user's profile in a short time.

Twitter is very popular among various users because the restriction of tweets to 280 characters promotes creativity among users. A user will need to look for the easiest way to communicate their message in short and simple sentences. Therefore, you only need a glance to go through the content on the platform.

How Does the Twitter Platform Function?
Setting up a profile on Twitter is free. Once you have an account, you can send tweets as often as you want. To create a tweet, you simply type in your message in the, "What's Happening" box. After clicking on the Tweet button, your message will be visible to other users, including those that follow your account and some that don't.

According to Twitter etiquette, when a user follows your account, you should follow back. There is a Twitter feed that displays your tweets, tweets from users you follow, retweets, and replies. The follow button is what makes the tweet from certain users appear on your Twitter feed; if you don't find value in the tweets of a user, you can choose the Unfollow option.

What You Should Understand About Twitter
Twitter is a platform that allows people to enjoy their freedom. There are various information, videos, and images that you will find on the platform. Depending on how you use the platform, Twitter can be a great place to gather knowledge, grow your personal brand, or get news updates.

Many Twitter users tweet as a form of recreation. It is a significant reason why a lot of tweets appear as self-promotion, vanity, or attention seeking posts. Amid all the nonsense you will find on the platform, useful content is also available.

Gaining access to content that you deem useful and valuable will require you to make the right choice when selecting users that you follow.

Tweets, Retweets, Hashtags, And Direct Messages

Twitter allows users to communicate using four major methods that include tweets, retweets, hashtags, and direct messaging. Understanding each of these methods is essential to the growth of your personal brand.

A tweet is a message you send that appears on the Twitter feed. You can also direct this message to a user by including an "@" symbol followed by the Twitter handle of the user. Depending on how you curate the tweet, you can get it to appear to followers of the user you are directing the tweet to alone or it can be visible to everyone on the platform.

A retweet is a simple way to share a tweet from a user with your followers. As a personal brand, it is an easy way to promote another brand to your followers. You can choose to add a message before the retweet or retweet directly. It is also an excellent way to share any information you find useful with your followers.

Any phrase or word that comes after a pound (#) symbol on Twitter is a hashtag. Users on Twitter use a hashtag to create a topic or subject of interest that other users can easily follow. All tweets containing a specific hashtag are grouped for viewing on Twitter.

Although most messages on Twitter are shared publicly in the form of tweets, there is also an option to send messages to a user privately. A private conversation with another user is known as direct messaging. A direct message can only be sent to users that initiate a private conversation, those that follow you, and those that opt-in to receive direct messages.

Why Is Twitter Valuable in Building A Personal Brand?

As a social media platform, Twitter offers numerous benefits to its users. In addition to being optimized for the mobile platform and opportunity for rapid response, there are other benefits that make Twitter great for building a personal brand.

It Is an Excellent Marketing Tool

After growing your personal brand, you need to look for ways to promote the services of your personal brand. Placing an advertisement on Twitter is an excellent way to attract the attention of modern users that are internet-savvy.

You may advertise seminars, consultation services, and brand products on the platform. It also offers a greater reach than traditional advertising methods since most individuals pay less attention to television advertisements nowadays.

It Offers an Opportunity to Increase Sales, Leads, And Boost Business Growth

The best way to grow a business is to get a lot of people to know about the business. There are various ways to get your business into the sights of potential customers. You may consider guest blogging, presenting at a live workshop, or speaking at an industry event. All these are excellent choices, but as a start-up, you may not get the opportunity to play a significant role in any of these activities.

Using Twitter for personal branding is an excellent way to establish yourself as an expert in the industry. Once you become an authority, people begin to have more faith in your ability to handle the projects they have to offer.

Create A Great Profile

Depending on how you create your profile, you can attract a lot of new followers to your account. It is a fundamental step that you should not underestimate. A great profile is the first impression a visitor will have about your personal brand.

There are various tips to help you develop a great Twitter profile. Follow the tips below to make the most of your profile:

- Upload a personal profile photo

- Include a cover photo

- Create a compelling Twitter bio

- Include links to other platforms, like your website or blog, that tells users more about yourself

When developing a personal brand, you will be growing your online presence on multiple social media platforms. To make it easy for your audience to find you on various platforms, you should use the same profile photo across all platforms. You should remember to change the picture regularly or at least once a year.

It is essential you change the profile photo of your account from the default graphic. Using a picture that is the same across all your social media channels also helps.

Selecting the Appropriate Twitter Handle

With so many users on the platform, finding a handle that matches your name will not be an easy task. Nonetheless, you must remember to select a handle that is easy to remember. A Twitter handle that is consistent with your name on other social platforms is preferable. The two most important features of the handle are that it is easily recognizable and consistent.

You can choose a handle that showcases what your brand is all about. It is also important you remember that changing your handle too often will be detrimental to your brand. Why? As a personal brand, you want people to quickly identify your handle anytime they see it. Change it too often, and this will become impossible to achieve.

The Twitter Biography

The biography on Twitter is a section where you include a piece of brief information about yourself and the brand. The bio appears below the profile photo, and it is a concise summary. The idea is to introduce yourself to your potential customers or audience in the simplest way you can think of.

To make the most of your Twitter bio, you should include links and keywords. A link in the bio can work as part of your strategy to redirect traffic to your other social media channels. It is a good idea to add a link that redirects users to the about page of your website. On this page, users can learn a lot more about you since there is no limitation in the number of characters you can use.

To ensure you are reaching the right audience, adding a keyword is essential. The keyword you choose should be relevant to your niche and industry. Adding hashtags also helps but remember, you are working with a limited number of characters.

Developing Your Personal Brand

To ensure that you are developing your brand on Twitter the right way, there are certain things you need to ensure you are doing. In this section, you will learn about some actions that can help in the growth of your personal brand.

Participate in Twitter Chats

A Twitter chat is a recurring event that takes place at the same time and day on a weekly basis. The chat provides the opportunity for you to connect with other users and engage with them. You can also obtain information that will be relevant to the growth of your brand and appeal to other users that can become followers.

Participating in a Twitter chat will connect you with a community of users that are within your industry or niche. Some of these users may be influencers that can promote your brand while others may be experts that can offer advice.

Offering value is the best way to get noticed in any Twitter chat community. If you consistently provide value to other users within the community, you may stumble upon an opportunity to become a guest on the Twitter chat. Becoming a guest on a Twitter chat can establish your brand as an authority.

There are many Twitter chats available, and some are very popular. Finding one that is suitable for your brand is very important.

Respond to Your Followers

Engagement on Twitter involves two parties. Anytime you tweet, your followers may post comments on this tweet. It is crucial you respond to these comments to show them that they are recognized.

A follower may also decide to mention you in a tweet. Responding to the mentions is a crucial step in promoting engagement. By mentioning you in their tweet, a user is promoting your brand to his/her followers. Remember, a mention is a conversation that is about your brand.

It is very easy to forget to respond to comments and mentions when you are occupied with a different task. In building loyalty, trust, and a relationship with your followers, providing a response can go a long way.

Tagging and Sharing

Sharing valuable information with your followers is one of your obligations as a personal brand. A lot of the information or articles you will be sharing with your followers may not be authored by you. In this case, you need to tag the author of anything you decide to share.

Sharing the work of another individual is a form of promotion that they will appreciate if you tag them as the original author. Tagging will also help boost the image of your personal brand.

Follow Twitter Accounts of Influencers and Leaders in Your Niche

The first step you should take towards connecting with influencers and industry leaders is to follow their accounts. Once you start following them, you can look for different ways to establish a connection.

Some actions that you can take to connect with these users includes the following:

- Sending a simple hello

- Responding to their tweets

- Helping them anytime they request it

- Retweeting their tweets

Link to Your Blog

If you don't have a blog, then you need to create one to make the most of your Twitter account. Since Twitter is a microblogging platform, then it is an excellent place to redirect traffic to your blog. The limitation in the length of a tweet makes it difficult to display your expertise.

Instead, you can use Twitter to develop a voice and share short information. You can then add a link to redirect users to a blog. On the blog, the information will complement whatever you share on Twitter.

Combining these two platforms effectively will promote massive growth.

Use Videos to Make A More Significant Impression
An excellent way for your brand to stand out on Twitter is through the effective use of videos. There are different ways you can create a video for Twitter.

To promote more engagement and make your followers feel important, you can choose to make a video in which you reply to some of their questions. You may also decide to create video content and redirect them to your channel on YouTube to view the full video. It is an excellent way to generate traffic on other social media platforms.

You will become more memorable to your followers if they can place a voice behind your tweets.

Remain Active and Tweet Regularly
Building a successful personal brand on Twitter will require a lot of experimentation on your part. The experimentation phase is usually during the initial launch of the Twitter account. You need to experiment to determine the best time to tweet.

Determining the best time to tweet doesn't mean that you should only tweet at this time. You need to be active throughout the day. Why? Twitter is a platform that anyone can access whenever they want. Therefore, while some of your target audience may check their Twitter feed in the morning, others may do so late in the evening. By remaining active throughout the day, you can interact with your target audience regardless of when they decide to log into their account.

Your ability to remain active is equivalent to consistency. For better and faster results, you need to be consistent in your approach.

Offer Value

Twitter is a lot more than posting tweets regularly. Your tweets must provide value to your followers if you want them to connect with your brand. In developing your brand, you should have other platforms through which you have established yourself as an authority. These can be on your blog or other blogs where you have done a guest post.

Sharing content that you have authored and content from other experts in the industry are excellent ways to provide value to your followers. A delicate balance is essential when sharing content.

The way you curate your tweet also has an impact on the value you are providing to your audience. If all your tweets are riddled with pessimism or negativity, a lot of people will stay away from your brand. Providing positive motivation or insights into a problem you are sure your audience is facing will impress your audience positively.

Remember, you must tag the author when sharing content that isn't yours and include images anytime it is possible.

Get Personal in Your Posts

Showcasing yourself as a human is one of the general ideas in developing a personal brand. Most members of your audience will find it easy to connect with your brand when they understand that you are also human. Uploading posts that share an element of humanity is essential.

Selfies, pictures with your dog, you and your employees preparing for an event, etc., are some personal posts you can upload.

Let the People You Follow Be Those That Are Active on The Platform

You won't get a lot from being active on Twitter if your followers and those you follow are not active. You may not have control over those that follow you, but you can at least select the users you decide to follow. When making your selection, it is crucial you consider those that are very active on the platform.

Having active followers will help you get a higher engagement rate on the platform. These users will help share your content and engage with the brand regularly. Another benefit of following other users is that it helps increase the number of followers you already have on the platform.

One of the basic Twitter etiquettes is to follow any user that follows you. The same will apply when you follow others.

Using Twitter Lists

If you want to organize your Twitter dashboard properly, then you should learn how to make use of Twitter lists. A Twitter list can help you separate the accounts of different users into different groups.

You may decide to create a list for customers of your brand and another for influencers within your niche. You can then choose to view only tweets from your customers using the customers list or of influencers using the influencers list.

Using this method, it is easier to first go through the tweets that you feel will be more significant to you on the platform before moving on to the general Twitter feed.

Make Use of Hashtags and Trends

In addition to the hashtags you create, you may also find hashtags under the trending topics on Twitter. A trending topic is one that is currently experiencing a lot of engagement from Twitter users. Hashtags are also popular in creating trends.

To make it easy to boost your personal brand, you can make use of hashtags when sending out a tweet. Using a trending hashtag will ensure that your tweet will be visible anytime someone searches for that hashtag.

Correct use of hashtags will make your content easy to find and help in making you a part of meaningful conversations.

Twitter Metrics You Need to Note

Metrics are necessary if you want to monitor the performance of your branding strategy on Twitter. There are different metrics that indicate the performance of your personal brand. Here are some of these metrics:

Reach and Mentions

The Reach on Twitter refers to the number of users that view your tweets or any tweet that includes a branded keyword. Mentions on Twitter cover various aspects. A public tweet from another user that includes your Twitter handle is a mention. A mention is also a tweet from any user that consists of any of your keywords.

There are Twitter analytics tools that assist in the analysis of tweets that include your keyword over a period. A clear indication that you are connecting with your target audience and providing content that they want is a high value of mentions and reach. It also means that your targeting strategy is working as your content is getting to the right audience.

Sentiment

The Twitter Sentiment is another important metric that you can find on specific analytics tools. The analysis of Twitter Sentiment involves the classification of actions regarding your brand into a neutral, positive, or negative action. You or other users may perform these actions.

This means you will be searching for positive and negative actions towards your personal brand. The growth of your personal brand on Twitter rides on not only a wider reach but also on mentions, services, products, and tweets that invoke positive sentiments on the Twitter platform.

Negative actions may be in the form of negative comments on your tweets or a negative tweet that mentions your Twitter handle. It is necessary you look for a way to resolve such issues. Getting negative comments is not a bad thing as it helps you build trust with other users. Perfection is not always a good sign for most social media users.

Engagement Rate

There are different aspects that an analytics tool will cover under engagement. Each element of engagement is a unique form of reaction that your tweets are generating from your followers. Your Twitter engagement report will include an analysis of the following aspects:

- Shares/retweets

- Likes

- Comments

If a follower is retweeting your content, then you should know that they believe in what you post. Such a follower has assessed your brand and concluded that your brand is credible. Engaging with such a follower will yield a positive result as they can quickly become loyal to the brand.

In general, a higher engagement rate means that more users will see your tweets. Therefore, getting more users to retweet, like, and comment on your tweets is essential for the growth of your personal brand.

Hashtag Performance

Finding a Twitter analytics tool that can assess the performance of hashtags on your page is essential. Hashtags are a necessary tool in promoting your brand and content.

For each campaign you want to run on Twitter, it is crucial you create a keyword that you can use as the hashtag for the campaign. Through an assessment of the hashtag, it will also be possible to assess the effectiveness and performance of any campaign on the platform.

An excellent analytics tool should be able to provide some vital information under the hashtag analysis such as:

- Interactions

- Estimated reach

- Number of mentions

It may also offer a list of trending hashtags as suggestions so you can find one to incorporate in a personal brand.

Things to Avoid When Building A Personal Brand on Twitter

In your quest to make the most of Twitter in your personal branding, you may end up making some mistakes that you ought to avoid. Learning some of these mistakes now can help you avoid them in the future. Here are some common mistakes people make when developing a personal brand:

Don't Give in To Twitter Trolls

Social media is a place where trolls thrive. Since it is easy for people to hide their identity, they can get away with almost anything. A Twitter troll is a Twitter account with the sole purpose of getting your attention through direct or indirect attacks on your brand. There is often no appropriate reason for these attacks.

Differentiating a complaint from a troll can be very difficult. In this case, the action you need to take is apparent. Remain responsible in the way you respond to other users or tweets.

Using the Number of Followers as An Indication of Success

If you are still making this mistake, then it means you don't understand the importance of the various Twitter analytics tools available.

In the early years of Twitter, the number of followers on a handle used to be a useful metric. Now, it doesn't matter as much.

There are other more important metrics that you should be monitoring. These include the following:

- Twitter Sentiment

- Engagement rate

- Leads generation

- Hashtag performance

You can use these metrics to assess the progress you are making in achieving the goals you have put in place for your personal brand.

Oversaturating the Twitter Feed of Followers

Increasing the frequency of your tweets can be a helpful growth strategy for your personal brand. It is also a method to show that you are active on the platform. Nonetheless, it still needs a bit of moderation.

If your audience starts getting fed-up by the number of tweets from your handle, they will take the easy way out. Yes, they will unfollow you. It is a simple way to get rid of the issue you are creating on their Twitter feed.

There are other actions you may be performing that will often irritate a follower. These actions include the use of slang, excessive promotional posts, failure to reply to messages, trying too hard to be funny, and a lack of personality behind the brand.

Taking note of changes in the engagement rate on your handle is essential. You may notice it in the form of a decrease in engagement while you are attempting an increase in the number of your daily posts.

Considering Your Tweets as A Temporary Action

When you feel you can always delete a tweet, it is easy to post content that will be inappropriate to most users. As a result, you may end up posting a tweet that goes against everything your brand is supposed to stand for.

With the advancement in technology, it is very easy for a user to take a screenshot of your tweet and use it against your brand in the future. To avoid this from happening, you need to review every tweet before posting it.

Don't give in to your emotions when replying to a customer or follower. Emotional responses often have a significant impact on your brand image. Always try to act professionally anytime you need to post so you can avoid publicizing anything that may damage the brand you are building.

Chapter 8:
Creating a Personal Brand on Instagram

What Is Instagram?

Instagram is a social media platform that connects users from around the world. It functions as a sharing app for photos and videos that is free to use. As an Instagram user, you have instant access to a personal news feed after sign-up. In this regard, you can liken it to other social media platforms like Twitter and Facebook. Other features available include the Explore tab that lets you find profiles that you may be interested in and other users close to your location.

You also have access to your profile that displays any video or photo you post on the platform while you can view posts from other users on your news feed. Your followers' news feed will also display the videos and photos you post on the platform. Interaction on Instagram involves tagging, commenting, sending a direct message, liking posts, getting followed, and following other users.

The unique feature of Instagram is the focus on the mobile platform. The Instagram platform is fully optimized for use on a mobile device so users can access their profile anytime and anywhere.

How Can I Access the Instagram Platform?

Instagram is compatible with various mobile devices. These include devices that operate on the Android operating system and those running on the iOS like the iPad and iPhone. Although its design and use focus on the mobile platform, it supports web access using a computer.

Importance of Instagram In Personal Branding

As a social media platform, Instagram offers a lot of features that make it great for building a personal brand. If you understand what you can gain, it makes it easier to invest the time and energy to build your brand. Below are some common benefits of Instagram:

Lead Generation

When developing a personal brand, having multiple social media platforms will be a great benefit. Promoting your various social media pages on other platforms is also an essential strategy for growth. On Instagram, you have the option of including a clickable link or URL in your profile bio.

Having a lot of followers on Instagram can help boost the growth or traffic on any other channel you connect using the embedded link.

It Improves Your Ranking on Search Engine Results

An Instagram page is a great way to promote your visibility online. Your followers, combined with high-quality content, increases your rank on search engine results. It is a great way to extend the reach of your personal brand.

Opportunity to Implement Numerous Hashtags

To ensure that you can reach users with similar interests, Instagram enables the use of hashtags on posts. To improve the effectiveness of hyper-targeting, it supports up to thirty hashtags on a single post. It also provides a means for location targeting depending on how you implement the hashtags.

Getting Started – Setting Up A Profile for Your Personal Brand

Following a strategy to guide your brand building process is essential for success. The first step to your success is by starting with a killer profile.

Go Simple with The Username

Simplicity is a favorable option when selecting a username for your profile. Using your name is a suitable choice for a personal brand. On most social media platforms, it is usually impossible to use your exact name as the username since it will often be taken.

What you need to do is to look for a username that is a very close match to your name. It should be something that your followers will be able to remember with ease. To make sure it is simple, you should avoid the use of numbers and symbols when coming up with the right username.

Make the Most of The Name Field

A name field that is separate from the username is another feature you need to use to your advantage when setting up your Instagram profile. Including keywords in the name field will help in getting your page noticed by other users.

How?

The words you include in the name field are searchable words. This means that if a user inputs any word that is in your name field into the search entry, your page will pop up among the results. Incorporating targeted keywords is a good step in getting more traffic.

The right keywords include words related to your products, niche, and anything else you promote. You need to ensure people can find your page with just vague information.

Bio Optimization Is Important

Similar to how you develop a first impression when meeting someone new, you also need to make an excellent first impression on any user visiting your page. On Instagram, your bio is the easiest way to make an excellent first impression. You have to make the most of the space available since it is limited.

A good strategy is to separate the bio into parts. There should be a part that explains who you are and who will be interested in the content on your page. Another part should give an insight into what you do and offer while the last part can simply provide information on how you achieve the objectives of your page.

In the few seconds a potential follower will take to go through the bio, you must get them to fall in love with your page. You need to keep improving and updating your bio regularly. These updates should reflect your real-life growth and development. This is vital since you are trying to build a personal brand.

Combining the Bio with The Link

Instagram provides each user with the option of including one link on their page. Since the link appears below the bio, you need to use it in a way that explains why a user should click on said link.

The number of characters available for a bio is only 150. Nonetheless, you can find excellent ways to make the most of these characters. One method of saving space is to make use of emojis with your text.

Developing a great call-to-action (CTA) will also be beneficial in getting users to click on the link you provide on your page. There are also various tools you can use in linking pages or products to a particular Instagram post. Learning to use these tools eliminates the need to change the link on your bio while enabling you to redirect users to different pages, websites, or blog posts.

Developing Your Personal Brand on Instagram

It is now time to get into the main event. How you go about building your personal brand on Instagram is crucial. Although there will be a few similarities with the process on other platforms, there are still some unique aspects on Instagram.

Creating A Strategy for Building Your Personal Brand on Instagram

Having a strategy is an essential part of building a successful personal brand on Instagram. A strategy will help in outlining the steps you should take that will produce the most impact on your personal brand. Some of the factors that you should consider when creating a strategy includes the following:

Scheduling

Following a schedule when uploading posts is a great way to promote consistency with your posts. The schedule should consist of the hashtags you will use, the frequency of posts, and the best times to post.

Setting Goals

What do you intend to gain by running the Instagram profile? It is an important question that you must answer if you want to provide direction for your profile. It will also help you curate great content for the profile.

Choosing A Niche

A niche is a small section of an industry. Selecting a niche in an industry will help simplify the process of building a personal brand. It is because you can focus on a smaller area of the industry and establish yourself as an authoritative figure. A niche also helps in monitoring the competition and other influencers with similar interests.

Identifying the Target Audience

When developing a plan for the content you'll be posting on your page, you must consider the individuals that will suit your target audience. Your target audience will also help you identify other Instagram accounts you can follow to help promote your page.

Reviewing Your Progress

A social media platform aims to grow your personal brand. To ensure you are making progress, you need to keep track of your growth. Reviewing your profile from time to time is essential. The review should include monitoring the new followers, engagement on comments, conversions, sales, and so on.

Authenticity Is Crucial

Your personal brand will only be successful if you can be yourself. If you think social media users will not notice a fake personality, then you will be in for a great surprise.

Growing your brand and remaining authentic may seem like a difficult task on Instagram. Nonetheless, there are lots of methods that can make your brand appear genuine to your followers. Here are some standard methods:

Focus on Your Niche Audience

There is a reason why you are selecting a niche for your brand. The way you handle your niche audience will differ from how you handle your audience from another niche. An easy way to become an inauthentic brand is by trying to please everyone.

How do you try to please everyone? If your niche audience has a more significant number of younger individuals, then you may decide to choose a brand voice that connects with these more youthful individuals. In a bid to please the older demographic, you may need to switch to a brand voice that is more professional.

When you select your target audience, ensure you focus solely on this audience. Do not waste any effort in trying to attract the wrong crowd.

Let Your Brand Voice Be Unique

Your brand voice should reflect your personality as an individual. Other aspects that complement the brand voice include the type of content you post, the tone you use in your content, and visuals you upload on your account.

An easy way to differentiate your brand from others is through your voice. Make your brand voice engaging and fun to your followers. Your ability to communicate and connect to your followers is one of the effects of an authentic brand voice.

A brand voice that will easily connect with your followers is one that can portray the humanity behind your brand.

Accept Negativity

Negativity often serves as a stepping stone for your growth. Show your audience that you are mature in the way you handle negativity on your account.

To promote authenticity, don't give in to the temptation of deleting negative comments. A brand that wants to portray a spotless image is telling its followers that it is hiding a lot. A more suitable approach is to provide a solution to the issue.

Organic Growth Is Crucial

If your account has a lot of followers, it becomes easier for new users to follow your account. During the initial development of your brand, you will not have a lot of followers. A lot of brands opt for an easier alternative – the purchase of fake followers.

Identifying such brands is very easy. An account with thousands of followers struggling to reach an average of fifty likes per post is not legitimate.

Organic growth is only possible if you offer value to other users. You are better off growing steadily by making a follower feel recognized than tricking them into following a brand that is undeserving. There are also lots of benefits you will enjoy from organic growth. These include building an active brand community as well as word-of-mouth recommendations.

Your Instagram Posts Should Have A Theme
Creating an Instagram account that is cohesive is crucial to the success of your personal brand. Your followers will quickly lose interest in your account if you are not consistent with your posts. A user that decides to follow your account due to a post about dogs will lose interest if you start making posts about gaming consoles.

The theme of your Instagram account is a lot more than the subject of your posts. You should also have some sort of color palette that is consistent with all your Instagram posts. Having a color palette will produce a beautiful appearance anytime a new user opens your profile.

Although it is crucial your posts follow the same theme, you may sometimes have to upload a post that will deviate from your usual posts. You have two options in this case. You can either look for a way to relate the post to the purpose of the account or upload such posts occasionally.

If your personal brand focuses on your love for games and gaming consoles, posting a photo of your trip to the Electronic Entertainment Expo (E3) is still relevant to the brand you are building.

Effective Use of Hashtags

Although hashtags are available for use as you see fit, you need to ensure you are using this powerful tool most efficiently. A hashtag can help you attract new followers with ease by promoting your content to users that have an interest in the content on your page.

Regardless of how effective they are, you may be overusing hashtags on your page. It is a common mistake most people make since it is free and allows for unrestricted access.

You will have seen a lot of people that overuse hashtags on their posts. These are posts that have over twenty hashtags with only two hashtags that are relevant to the original post.

If you want your hashtags to make the most impact, you should use about seven hashtags at most on a single post. Remember, this is a recommendation, not a rule.

If you select the right hashtags that can get your content to individuals within your niche, target audience, and other users, you are going to see a lot of growth.

Create A Network

As a brand, you also need to connect with other brands and influencers within your niche. By connecting with these brands and influencers, you can create a network that can help grow your brand.

By following other influential users within your niche, you can learn about upcoming events that can help promote your brand. Connecting with other influencers on a personal level will also provide the opportunity for them to give you a shout out on their page and promote your brand to their followers.

Redirect Traffic to Your Other Social Media Channels

There is a limit to the information you can share on your Instagram page. The limit can be easy to notice since the platform is solely for photo and video sharing. To make the most of the follower growth on your Instagram, you need to ensure you are redirecting your followers to your other social media channels.

A simple mention of your blog, website, Facebook group, or Twitter handle will help you promote traffic on these channels. Since there is the option of including only a single bio link, you need to make the most of every opportunity that is available to you.

You can also combine individual posts with the bio link. Are you having a giveaway? You can make a post where you mention the giveaway and tell users to click on the bio link to get more information. Using free tools like Linktree will help you make the most of the single bio link on the account.

Sometimes, it may become essential to use your bio link to promote the sales of a product by redirecting users to the product page. It is vital you don't do this frequently. The reason is quite simple. While you may be promoting product sales, you may not be improving the brand loyalty of your customers by pushing products.

Implement Geotags

A location tag that you include on an Instagram post is called a geotag. The location is the latitude and longitude of the position of the mobile device that is currently logged into the Instagram account.

To use the geotag feature, Instagram needs to receive permission to make your location public. Including a location on the content you post makes it easier to connect with users around the same area.

There are various features of Instagram geotags that you should know about. These include:

Instagram Story Sticker

Using the geotag as the basis, Instagram can consist of a digital sticker on your Instagram stories.

Location Hashtags

If you understand the effectiveness of a hashtag when sharing content that is relevant to a niche, then it is easy to understand location hashtags. These hashtags consist of a location as the keyword. The hashtag, #Dallas, is a simple example. You can also use location hashtags in the form of stickers on your Instagram stories.

Using the location hashtags makes it easy to connect with other users that are within the same location.

Location Creation

The location creation option is a feature that you can take advantage of if there is no geotag location available for you. The only downside to the location creation is the fact that it is only possible on Facebook.

As soon as your setup the location on the Facebook platform, it becomes visible on the Instagram platform.

In addition to being easy to use, Instagram geotags also promote easy connection and relationship development between your audience and your brand. The option of including a geotag using a single click makes them very easy to use.

Providing a location when making a post makes it easy for your followers to connect with you. Fans will love to meet up for lunch with the person running their favorite Instagram account if they get the opportunity.

Edit and Improve Photos or Images Using Apps

One of the unique features of Instagram is the inclusion of filters to enhance your photos. As a photo-sharing platform, your success will depend mainly on the quality of the images you upload.

The authenticity of your posts, geotags, and hashtags that you implement will not have any effect if the quality of your posts are poor. Using a lousy filter will only make things worse.

A lot of Instagram filters are "cliché." In place of these filters, you can opt for photo editing apps that will provide a natural look to your photos while enhancing the quality. You may also use apps like Photoshop if you have Photoshop knowledge.

All Comments on Your Posts Need A Reply

To grow your personal brand, you want your audience to connect with you. To promote this connection, engagement is essential. Responding to each comment you get on your post is a great way to encourage engagement and build a relationship with your audience.

You may be getting up to fifty comments on each post but replying with a simple "thank you" to each comment will show that your audience is important to you. If you are getting responses from trolls, then you can choose to ignore these comments.

As a growing personal brand, you don't have an excuse for not replying to all the comments. Only an Instagram page with followers entering into the thousands can get away with not responding to all the comments on a post.

Include A Call for Engagement

Promoting engagement is necessary for growth. A call for engagement is simply a question you ask after uploading a post that will result in audience engagement in the form of comments. You can curate content that will require audience engagement to make it meaningful.

There are lots of questions you can ask your audience to trigger engagement. Some simple questions include the following:

- What is your morning exercise routine like?

- On a scale of 1 – 10, how effective is this product?

- How are you planning to enjoy the Premier League matches this weekend?

- How are you preparing for the final season of Game of Thrones?

You can also promote engagement by getting your followers to tag their friends. Tagging is another excellent way to promote your page to other users through your followers.

Promote Other Brands on Your Page

Many brands on social media keep searching for new individuals that will become loyal audience members. If you choose to promote the

Instagram page of other brands, they will be obliged to do the same for your brand.

Choosing to promote a brand with a large number of followers will help you reach a large target audience when they decide to return the favor.

An essential part of getting other brands to review your videos or photos is to provide high-quality content. High-quality content can captivate a new audience, establish authority, and increase your number of followers.

Providing Some Personal Information

A crucial difference between a personal brand and a business brand is how they operate. A business brand needs to operate with a level of professionalism while a personal brand should be willing to get personal with the clients.

Providing details of your personal life is a requirement for the growth of your personal brand. Your goal is to avoid growing an Instagram account that your followers will see as a means for you to make money.

The personal details you may share can include photos from your last vacation, your daily exercise routine, and so on.

Important Growth Metrics to Monitor

Metrics are vital statistics that help you assess the growth of your Instagram page as well as your brand. These metrics are also essential in evaluating the success of your Instagram strategy to identify areas that may require a new approach.

Some of the metrics you should look out for include the following:

Impressions

The number of Instagram users that see a post on your page is known as impressions. It is an excellent way to evaluate the success of your strategy for content promotion. The strategy includes the use of trends and hashtags on the platform.

The posts that make up the impressions on your page include those that do not have any likes or comments from users. A useful tool for checking impressions is through Instagram Insights.

Users Rate of Engagement

Various actions make up the engagement rate on your Instagram account. These include the number of shares, likes, saves, shares, and comments on the posts on your account.

In building your personal brand, you need to pay close attention to comments from your users when growing the account. A lot of these comments offer feedback. The feedback from users can help you identify areas that need improvement. It is also essential you reply to the comments on your page.

Although you can look at the engagement rate for all the posts on your page, reviewing the engagement for each post has its benefits. In this form of assessment, you can identify the post with the highest rate of engagement. The information can help in determining the type of content your users love to see.

You can also use the engagement rate analysis to identify an influencer that will be beneficial in your influencer marketing strategy. You can also find industry standard guidelines that you can use in assessing your engagement rate performance.

Bio Link Click-Throughs

Instagram provides one clickable link, and that is the bio link. Effectively using your bio link can help promote sales of a product or drive traffic to another page. When building your personal brand, you can use the bio link to redirect your followers to a blog page, website, product page, etc.

The bio link click-throughs help in identifying the number of users that click on the bio link.

Follower Growth

Is your content attracting new users to your page? It is the fundamental question the follower growth metric answers. The follower growth metric is a more suitable option in assessing the ability of your content to captivate your target audience.

Using the follower growth rate to assess the effectiveness of your marketing strategy will not provide accurate results. You need to understand that while you may be getting your content across to your target audience, members of the audience may not find value in the content that will prompt them to follow your page.

Metrics for Your Instagram Stories

Instagram Stories are posts that appear for just 24 hours before they disappear. These stories can either be photos or videos but are useful as a marketing tool. You may not get as much information as you require to assess the effectiveness of your stories, but you can make do with what is available. Below are some of the metrics available.

Completion Rate

This is an indication of the number of users that view the complete story you post. It is a percentage that you have to calculate using the users that saw the first story and those that saw the last story. Dividing the latter by the former and then multiplying by 100 will provide the percentage you need.

Direct Messages

You can determine a percentage of the engagement rate using the Direct Messages (DM) you receive from the Instagram stories. Simply divide the number of messages by the number of views and multiply it by 100. The result gives you the engagement rate of a story.

Views

It is merely the number of users that viewed your story. The views will vary for each story you upload which is why the completion rate is often lower than 100 percent.

If you want to compare the Instagram Stories metrics at different times, you will need to keep personal records since it is not available on the platform.

The Most Suitable Time and Day to Upload New Posts

On a lot of Instagram pages, the quality of the content does not affect the engagement rate. You may find that you are having low engagement rates on some of your posts while others have very high engagement rates. It may be a result of the time or day you decide to upload your post.

Understanding your target audience can help determine the best time for you to post and the best day. If you have a lot of followers in a time zone that is 6 hours behind yours, uploading a post at 8 a.m. in your time zone might mean it's 2 a.m. in your target audience's time zone. Six additional hours is enough time for other users to create posts that will push yours further down the feed.

Hashtags

Underestimating the power of hashtags will ruin your chances of success on Instagram. If you understand the importance of keywords when creating content on a website, then you can liken these keywords to hashtags.

Since hashtags are essential, you should know that your competitors will also be incorporating hashtags into their posts. Identifying the hashtags that perform the best in promoting engagement and those that have a lot of followers is essential.

Creating hashtags that are unique to your brand is also essential. You can then monitor these hashtags to find users that are making use of them. It is a simple way to identify loyalty and users that are fans of the brand. Going through the hashtags on the profile of your competitors is crucial. You may end up finding some hashtags that are performing excellently.

Hashtags can improve your engagement rate and impressions if you put them to excellent use.

Apps and Tools That Can Help with Building Your Personal Brand on Instagram

When creating your brand on Instagram, monitoring your growth and performance is crucial to your success. Using some of the tools available for this purpose will ease the process and also improve your efficiency. Some of the tools available include the following:

Grum

Grum is a web-based platform that allows a user to create a schedule for uploading their Instagram posts. It is an excellent tool for anyone that already has content that will help grow the social media presence of the personal brand.

The use of Grum is more effective if most of the content you intend to share is available on your computer, and not on a mobile device where it would be easy to access.

Grum allows you to create a strategy through which you can make a schedule for the post you will upload, the comments, and caption you will include on each post beforehand, so it is easy to upload on a particular date.

Owlmetrics

Owlmetrics is a tool that allows you to gather the necessary data to use in analyzing the performance of your Instagram page. The information it provides includes the engagement on your posts and Instagram stories, follower growth, and the most suitable time for uploading a post.

Canva

As an individual developing a personal brand, you may want to avoid hiring the services of a professional designer. Canva is a design tool that assists you in creating quality images that you can post on your page. You can also edit media files using this easy to use tool.

Linktree

The option of including only a single clickable link on your Instagram bio can be somewhat limiting to your brand growth. If you need an option to redirect your followers to multiple pages, then Linktree is the tool you should be using.

With Linktree, you can create a landing page to which users will be redirected to if they click on the bio link. On this landing page, you can include various links for different parts of your website or other social media channels you want your followers to visit.

Union Metrics

A platform that helps assess the performance of your Instagram account is the Union Metrics. Most of the information you get on this platform may appear basic, but they can be beneficial in making some critical changes to your account.

The information and report provided from the platform can quickly help you determine the type of content your followers enjoy, the content they don't like, the most suitable hashtags to incorporate, and the best time to upload a post for the best result. An excellent feature of the platform is the indication of your top follower in the report. The identification of this follower is a reminder that it is essential you interact with them regularly.

How to Use the Union Metrics Report

Signing up on the Union Metrics platform is a requirement to get the free report. To create an account, all you need is an email and a password. Once you provide these details, you should then permit Union Metrics to access your Instagram account information.

To provide an accurate report, Union Metrics will need some time to gather information from the account. It is a process that will appear in the form of a wait screen or a progress screen.

As soon as the platform extracts the necessary information, you can view the report that will be displayed. The data on the report is from the previous month.

Some of the information you can find on the report includes your top hashtag, the best time and day to upload a post, your biggest fan, the post with the most engagement, and the post with the least engagement.

If viewing the report on your screen is not enough, you can choose to share or download a copy of the report.

Squarelovin

This is another free tool that provides Instagram analytics for free. It also includes information in the form of insights that can help in optimizing your Instagram page. The information available consists of the worst time to upload a post on Instagram. The reports on this tool appear in a straightforward format.

Using the Squarelovin Platform

To be able to use the tools available on Squarelovin, it is necessary you sign up on the platform. Upon activation of the account via an email, your sign up will be complete. You can then add an Instagram account.

There are various statistics available on the platform, and you can gain access to them through the dashboard. Opening the multiple tabs feature will show you different statistics with detailed information.

To view and analyze information of the comments and likes on your account, you can click on the Engagement tab. You will also be able to identify the post with the most comments and the most likes.

The Postings tab is another great feature you might want to check out. It provides information about your top posts as well as the post history of the account. To make it easier to assess your growth over time, the posts appear on a year, month, day, and time basis.

To find out what time of day is best to upload a new post, you can visit the optimization tab. The best day for posting is also indicated here.

Other features that you can find on the platform includes your Instagram Hashtags history and analysis, filter analysis, and the worst time to post and on what days.

These features are easily accessible on the left sidebar of the dashboard.

Chapter 9:
How to Capitalize on Personal Branding

To be considered a successful personal brand on social media, your brand has to have gone through the essential phases with positive results. In this regard, your brand will have a massive following that is inclusive of members of your target audience. These followers are those that can identify the value in your personal brand.

Up until this moment, all you have done is provide value, grow your brand, establish the brand as an authority, and engage with the audience. These are some of the essential steps to becoming a successful personal brand. Another critical step is how you can make money and generate revenue through your personal brand.

There are various ways through which you can make money using your brand. Read on to find out more about the available methods.

Make Money Promoting the Products of Another Brand or The Brand Itself

It is a popular and straightforward way to make money through the personal brand you have built. You are going to work with a brand in promoting its products to your audience or promote the brand itself. It is a method that requires the use of your influence on social media platforms like blogs, Twitter, YouTube, Instagram, Facebook, etc.

Depending on your niche and the influence of your personal brand, you may have several businesses reaching out to you. They do so to enjoy the benefits of your influence in boosting their product sales. It is also an excellent strategy to reach out to other smaller businesses you may know within your locality.

All you need to do in this case is to promote the product of the brand to your followers. You may achieve this goal by giving a review of the products the business is selling or the services they offer. To make sure you are giving an honest review, these businesses will provide a sample product for you to test or provide a free service at any one of their outlets that is closest to you.

There are a few things you should avoid. The first is to ensure you pick a credible brand to promote. Any issue with the brand is sure to affect your relationship with your followers. Another critical thing to avoid is oversaturating your page with promotional advertisements. Following a schedule can help you overcome this issue.

You can also find websites and apps that make it easy to connect with brands that need your services in promoting their products. Most of these websites and apps provide brand requirements so you can assess to find those that suit your brand. You may also need to create content that the brand can go through to determine if you are a great match or not.

Affiliate Marketing

If you want to earn passive income after building a personal brand, affiliate marketing is an excellent option. In this form of marketing, you receive a link through which you can receive commission. To make money through the link, which is also the affiliate link, your followers need to make a purchase after clicking on the link. The commission you are entitled to receive is simply a percentage of the sales made to users that visit an e-commerce platform through your link.

To become an affiliate marketer, you need to join an affiliate program. There are various affiliate programs available, and a popular program involves you becoming an Amazon Associate. As an Amazon Associate, the affiliate links you receive and the products you promote will be from Amazon.

You can also find other affiliate programs through sites like Click bank. Depending on your niche, you can find a product from the collection of products available. Ensure you read the Terms & Conditions of a program to confirm your eligibility and how you should promote the product.

To make sure you can get a commission on the sales of a product, your first step is to determine how to get your audience to make a purchase. The simplest way is to write a high-quality review. Within the content, you can embed your affiliate links.

Emails and banner ads can also be used in promoting your affiliate links. To provide an honest opinion on any product you are promoting, be sure to provide both the pros and cons of the product to your audience. You must be trustworthy unless your audience will not be willing to make purchases.

Your audience should be able to identify an affiliate link as an ad in your content. You should also know that certain niches offer a higher commission on product sales.

Create and Sell Informational Products

Becoming an authority in a niche or field has its benefits. Since it is a process that takes a reasonable amount of time, you would have developed and gathered a lot of knowledge about the niche. It is now time to put the knowledge to good use.

There are different ways to make money from selling informational products. Creating an eBook or an online course are two of the more common methods available. You can visit websites like Coursera and Udemy to create online courses to sell to visitors. It is also possible to provide these courses directly to your audience on your blog or other social media platforms.

You can also write an eBook to provide a large amount of information to your audience in a book format. Interested members of your audience can purchase the eBook directly from your social media pages, website, or blog. These purchases are usually much better since you don't need to pay commission for using any platform.

Amazon Kindle Direct Publishing is a platform that can also make it easier to create and sell an eBook. It is straightforward to access the platform from any device you own. Using this platform will mean you have to pay a percentage to Amazon on the sales you make.

EBooks that are easy to read, non-fiction, with lots of value to the readers sell faster. Asking for a review from your readers will also help in improving your sales.

If you think that creating an online course will be a more desirable option, then you should determine the best means of getting returns on any course you create. The following are some of the methods you can use to turn in profits:

Request A Fee for Certification While Offering A Free Course
There are lots of reasons why this model will turn in profits. Firstly, you can attract a lot of people to the course since they don't have to worry about the cost of enrollment. Secondly, you can create an email list from the details of individuals that enroll in your online course.

The final reason is that certification has value to individuals in building a career. As a result, they are willing to pay for anything that will boost their progress.

Create A Tier System

For an online course to be successful, you have to provide value that is difficult to get and a price that is difficult to match. By creating a tier system, you can offer the first tier for free while the other tiers will be available for a fee.

If an individual goes through the free tier and finds valuable information, they will be willing to pay for access to the advanced content you have to offer.

Up-Front Course Payments

The standard form of payment that is in place in educational institutions is the up-front payment. You pay for whatever you want to learn beforehand. Your audience will be familiar with this form of payment.

There are reasons why this form of payment may be more beneficial. With this form, there is an extent to which the payment covers. You don't have any obligation to offer anything beyond the content of the course an individual has paid. On the other hand, offering a subscription payment means that individuals can access as much information as possible during the period of subscription.

Subscription

Providing a subscription can be beneficial to your audience since they can simply stop making payments as soon as they cease to find value in what you offer. Regardless, it may also be more challenging to get people to pay for a subscription. This is because a lot of people believe that you may not be able to provide value that will match the sub-scription fees.

Pre-Selling Courses

Pre-selling is an excellent idea since it is your audience funding the project. It doesn't cost you money, no reason to wonder if you will make sales, and no guessing what topic to write on. These are just a few benefits of pre-selling.

By pre-selling a course, you are making a course on a topic you know your audience will want to learn more about. You can determine the topic through a simple poll. Once the survey is complete, you can get the audience to pay for the creation of the course through a fund-raising campaign.

The inability of the campaign to raise the necessary funds will be a good sign that you shouldn't create the course.

Get A Company That Is Willing to Purchase Licenses to Courses

In this case, the image of your brand as an authority will be useful. All you need to do is to create an online course, sell the license, and make money collecting the annual licensing fee on the course.

Marketing is vital in this case, but you will find a lot of companies that are willing to buy the license for a course. The customer service and technical aspects will be in the hands of the company.

Make Money from Consultation or Coaching Services

One of the major benefits of a personal brand on social media is access to your audience. The audience will include people that will be willing to pay for the services you offer and learn directly from you.

Coaching and consultation services gain a lot from personal branding. By building an audience and establishing your expertise, it is much easier to charge people that want to get more insight.

You may have established yourself as an expert in music. Your expertise may cover areas like playing musical instruments, reading and writing sheet music, making beats, or repairing instruments. A customer that wants to learn more about sheet music may decide to reach out to you for a coaching service. The service can be online, and you will receive payment for each session.

Having a course or an eBook that you can sell also works in combination with a consultation or coaching service. If a customer is consulting you on your expertise, be sure not to undersell. Charge customers for the value you offer.

Making Money from YouTube

There are different ways to make money using YouTube. All these methods are only lucrative if you have a lot of people subscribed to your channel. Below are some of the processes through which you can make money on YouTube.

Becoming A Member of The YouTube Partner Program

The YouTube Partner program opens lots of opportunities for you to make money on your YouTube channel. Getting approval to become a part of the program means you can try out different options to monetize your channel. Your approval will largely depend on your audience and your compliance with the policies of the YouTube Partner Program.

You will need to allow monetization on your channel to start making money on YouTube. You can find this option in the "Video Manager" section of your YouTube channel.

Below are some of the options available to you for making money through YouTube:

Merchandise

This includes mugs, t-shirts, pens, and other items that can help promote your YouTube channel. YouTube now allows channels to display their merchandise below their videos through the Teespring integration. You should follow the YouTube Community Guidelines to ensure your merchandise is in line with what is stated.

It is also possible to link the channel to a merchandise site that is approved on the platform.

Channel Memberships

Viewers on your channel can decide to pay an amount as a fee for Channel Membership. It is a recurrent fee that they will have to pay monthly. As a member, viewers can get access to some unique features. These include custom perks, unique emojis, special badges, and specific posts.

Other features include using your end screen or video card to create a link to any crowdfunding site approved by YouTube. To be able to provide the channel membership feature to your viewers, your channel must meet specific requirements and be in any of the supported locations.

Ads

Advertising remains one of the essential revenue sources on most social media platforms. YouTube also allows channels to place ads to generate revenue. Depending on your settings, the amount of revenue you can get will vary. Some key settings to ensure you are making the most out of the YouTube ads includes the following:

- Implementing targeting tools for proper ad placement. The tools enable audience targeting using interests, previous video interactions, or demographics.

- Enabling all the available ad formats and monetizing all future uploads.

- Uploading videos that are suitable for all audiences to avoid age restrictions. Videos that have an age restriction don't get monetized using ads.

- Effectively utilize video metadata such as title, description, tags, and thumbnail.

YouTube Premium

Placing Ads provides a substantial amount of income on a YouTube channel. So, what happens if a viewer doesn't want your ads to appear? These users can use the YouTube premium feature.

YouTube premium allows the user to offer support to your channel in exchange for ads-free viewing of your channel. They also have access to other features like offline viewing of videos through downloads. It is a form of paid membership, and the number of members viewing your content determines your earnings.

Brand Deals

If you can build a popular YouTube channel with a large number of subscribers, then you may have the opportunity to work with certain brands. These brands need your channel, so your viewers can learn about their products and services. To gain this market exposure, they will be willing to pay you to have you advertise or review their products on their channel.

It may also be a form of endorsement or sponsorship. Nonetheless, be sure to follow the YouTube guidelines.

Super Chat

Depending on your location, your channel may support the Super Chat feature on YouTube. Super Chat provides revenue to your channel since a viewer has to purchase this feature to use it during a live chat. During the chat, any viewer that uses the Super Chat feature can send a message that will be highlighted in the chat.

Another critical thing to remember is how you handle sensitive or controversial topics on your channel. If you want to remain on the YouTube partner program, you should remember to disable ads on specific videos. By removing ads on specific videos, you can ensure that only advertiser-friendly videos are monetized using ads.

Like other social media platforms, you can also engage in YouTube affiliate marketing to generate revenue. You can include your affiliate links in the video description or using annotations. Uploading unboxing, instructional, or review videos can help with affiliate marketing.

Google AdSense

This is a program that is available to blogs, YouTube channels, and websites. It allows individuals to run an ad on any one of these platforms to earn money anytime a member of their audience clicks on the advertisement.

Google AdSense is a great way to generate money from your personal brand, but it is crucial you gather a lot of information on the program to ensure you are using it right. The AdSense program is free and easy to join with various ad options available. Nonetheless, you can easily lose your AdSense account if you fail to follow the guidelines. Having steady traffic is an essential part of earning revenue using the program.

The ad types available include Flash, Audio, Text, Images, and so on. There is a minimum requirement of $100 for users that want to withdraw their earnings from the program and payment is made monthly. You need to be careful not to drive traffic using special programs.

There are some terms you need to learn if you want to take advantage of the Google AdSense program. These include the following:

Cost Per Click (Cpc)
It is the amount you earn for each click an ad receives on your page. The amount may vary depending on the advertiser.

Click-Through Rate (Ctr)
It is the division of the number of ads clicks by the individual ad impressions. It is given as a percentage. The ad impression refers to

the number of ads you have on a page. A page with 5 AdSense ads has 5 ad impressions.

Chapter 10:
Google Search with Personal Branding SEO

What Is Search Engine Optimization (SEO)?

The idea and the steps you take to improve the visibility of a website, blog, or social media channel when creating content online is known as Search Engine Optimization, or SEO for short. The visibility of the site, blog, or other social media channels usually refers to its ranking on the organic results of a search engine when users input a keyword.

Why Should You Bother with Personal Branding SEO?

The visibility of your social media channels, websites, or blogs depends on how well you can meet the various criteria search engines use in ranking their results.

By understanding personal branding SEO, you can improve the ranking of your pages to the top of the search engine results anytime a user inputs a keyword that is specific to your niche. Learning about the various personal branding SEO tactics is beneficial since it can help you in creating content that will be search engine friendly. Content that is search engine friendly will be easy to find on search engines like Google, be of high-quality, and also help in promoting your brand.

How Is Your Content Ranked on A Search Engine?

Various factors are considered by a search engine when ranking content on a search result. All these factors are put into algorithms that undergo continuous updates. These updates are essential to ensure that the results are ones that are relevant to the keyword and offer the best quality to the users.

Going over all the factors that a search engine uses in ranking your page is not the best solution. Instead, you should consider some of the critical factors and optimize your content to meet these factors.

The next section will cover some of the factors you need to pay attention to when performing your personal branding SEO.

SEO Factors on Your Page

The SEO factors in this category are those that appear on the actual website page. These are some of the factors that are easy to control if the content you upload on the website belongs to you.

In building your personal brand, you need to fully understand and master each of these factors to boost your online reputation and improve your personal branding strategy. The SEO factors that you can find on your page include:

The Quality and Length of Your Text-Based Content

To ensure you are getting the best result under this factor, you must create high-quality content. High-quality content is content that is original, well researched, and well written.

The length of the content is also essential. There is no specific number for the length of your content, but it is vital that it is elaborate and offers necessary and relevant information.

Your content must be free of plagiarism and bad grammar. These are some of the things that search engines can quickly identify. By ensuring you optimize each aspect in this case, you can quickly boost your ranking on search engines.

Relevance

Actions that indicate that the site is active is crucial in personal branding SEO. By updating the content that is available on the website with topics that are relevant to the keyword, you can improve the ranking of the site. Updates should be frequent and can be on a daily, weekly, or monthly basis.

The Structure of The Site

When building a website, various codes help to produce the final output. The codes that are used are also referred to as computer languages, and they can be either front-end or backend. Common examples of the codes in use include PHP, HTML, JavaScript, and CSS.

Communication between your computer and the search engine is done using these codes. The quality of the content on your site will not matter if the structure of the site is in disarray. The structure of the site is crucial for effective communication between the website and the search engine.

There are various ways you can address this issue. One of the methods is to include a sitemap on the website during its design. An easier option is to use WordPress when creating your website. The benefit of WordPress is that it eliminates any communication issues between the search engines and your website that may be a result of poor structuring.

Placement of Important Information

On a website, there are some areas that are given priority over others by a search engine. To boost your visibility, including valuable information in these areas will be beneficial in your personal branding SEO.

Some of these areas are on the front-end while others are on the backend. These include the page headings, URL, meta tags, title tags, descriptions, heading tags, and so on.

As you try to optimize each of these areas, you should make sure that the information you are including makes sense. While you are gunning for a boost in your search engine results, there are also search engine penalties that may affect your rankings.

Keywords

A keyword is a unique word that an individual will enter in the search entry to find content from your website. There are various keywords you can use, and these keywords have a significant impact on your personal branding SEO.

The keyword you pick needs to be used in the content you are creating. You should also include the keyword in the metadata. If you overuse a keyword, it may hurt your ranking. In the case of personal branding SEO, your keyword should be your name.

Remember, you need to be wary of the keyword density to avoid any accidental penalties. Only use it where it fits.

SEO Factors That Are Off the Page

These are other factors that are not on the actual website page. An example of this factor is given below:

Backlinks or Inbound Links

A backlink is also known as an inbound link. It is a type of hyperlink that is incoming to the webpage from a different website. Be extra careful when making use of backlinks on your website.

You may end up getting penalized if the tactics you are using to get backlinks appear to be unethical. Organic backlinks remain a beneficial tool that you should be using. Just make sure that it is from a website that is of high-quality and authoritative.

Your SEO Strategy

It is always a good idea to develop a strategy for your personal branding SEO to make yourself visible on search engines like Google. Nonetheless, you must ensure that the plan you develop doesn't violate any rules.

You may get penalized if the search engine considers your SEO strategy to be a black hat strategy. Black hat SEO strategies include any strategy that is designed solely to meet the criteria for a high ranking on a search engine without any regard for meeting the expectations of the human audience. Websites that use these strategies include those that rank high on search engine results but don't have any content worth viewing.

Black hat SEO strategies are not in compliance with the regulations of search engines. As search engines undergo updates and improvements, they keep getting better in differentiating black hat sites from trustworthy and authoritative websites.

If you are still not sure of strategies that fall within the domain of black hat strategies, then these examples should give you an idea:

- Link stuffing

- Paid links

- Hidden text

- Cloaking

- Top heavy

- Keyword stuffing

To avoid getting penalized or blacklisted from Google, avoid using any of these SEO strategies. You should also avoid hiring anyone for your personal branding SEO if they give you the promise of excellent results in a short time.

Create A LinkedIn Profile

In developing your brand, creating a detailed LinkedIn profile is a great way to enhance your visibility on Google. There are specific fields that you must fill because they are visible in the form of snippets when the search results appear on Google. These fields include the name, location, and position.

Creating a custom URL for a public profile is also helpful as you can include your name in the URL. You must also take advantage of links when completing the profile to redirect users to your blog, Twitter account, etc.

You can also create a profile on other professional networking platforms to further boost your personal branding SEO.

Developing A Personal Website

Another place online where you can populate information about yourself is on your website. You should make a profile on your website that will serve as the primary source of all information that a viewer will need.

If you have other social media channels, there should be a link that redirects users back to this page on your website. You should also include your name in the URL. Analytics on your website can give you a better understanding of how your audience is engaging and interacting with your personal brand.

Become an Authority in Your Field

If you want to boost your personal branding SEO, then one of the best ways to achieve this is by becoming an authority in your area of expertise. The factors that people assess before regarding you as an authority include the type and quality of content you publish online, the credibility of any website that has a backlink to your website or blog, as well as various social signals like mentions on Twitter and reposts of your articles.

There are other ways to establish yourself as an authority. You can do so by running a blog, guest blogging, making online presentations, press releases, customer testimonials and reviews, online presentations, and a few others. You should ensure that you don't restrict the type of content you publish to just a single format. Your content should include texts, images, videos, and audio formats.

Having Your Brand Appear on Multiple Platforms

If you google your name as your brand, how many sites appear in the search results? It is one of the most straightforward steps to take, and all you need to do is to become active on various platforms that users consider as 'authority' sites. An authority site is any site that some of the top individuals within your niche or industry respect for the high-quality content they offer.

Another major benefit of an authority site is the fact that search engines usually rank these sites very high on the search results. By getting your content to appear on these sites, it means that the content you offer is high-quality and valuable to other users.

Making Online Presentations

Sites like Scribd and SlideShare allow users to upload a presentation to their platforms. The presentation may be a speech at a seminar, workshop, or conference. Other users can then read your presentation and download it if they wish.

It is another easy way to boost your personal branding SEO as you can use it to establish yourself as an expert.

Guest Blogging

Guest blogging is an activity in which you post content on the blog of another user that is closely related to your niche. There may be specific blogs that are considered the top within your niche and they will usually rank high on the search results. You can get permission to write a guest post for these blogs to boost your SEO.

One of the benefits of guest posting is the opportunity for your content and personal brand to appear on multiple sites. You can also do interviews for these blogs if an opportunity arises.

SEO Penalties

As you try to perform your personal branding SEO, there are certain tactics you need to avoid if you don't want to get penalized. Search engines, like Google, impose SEO penalties if they deem your tactics to be black hat. You can group these penalties into two categories. They include:

Total Penalty

If you get a total penalty, it means that your site will no longer appear on the search engine. By removing the site from the search engine index, it will no longer need to consider your site for any search entry. You can also refer to it as a ban or de-indexing.

Partial Penalty

A partial penalty means that the search engine will still rank your site in a search engine result, but in comparison to your past rankings, the current rankings will be abysmal. In this case, you still have an opportunity to turn a new leaf before you receive a total ban.

How Does Google Impose A Penalty?

There are two ways through which Google imposes its SEO penalties on any site that it considers to be using black hat tactics. These include the following:

Through Algorithm

It is the software that determines how the search engine should rank a site in the first place. Regardless, it can also decide if a site has used a tactic that falls within the black hat domain in a bid to improve its rankings.

Manually

The manual method of imposing SEO penalties involves using a team of individuals to assess various websites. If there are certain aspects of the site that these individuals find unethical, they can decide to impose a penalty on the website. The team that Google employs for this purpose is the web spam team.

If you think you are above getting an SEO penalty, you can get a better picture of how seriously it takes its policies when you consider that the company imposed a penalty on itself (Angotti, 2012).

Chapter 11:
Powerful Personal Branding Secrets

Personal branding secrets are simple elements of a personal brand building strategy that give the assurance of success. As simple as they may sound, they have a significant impact on your personal brand growth depending on how they are incorporated. These secrets include:

Your Personal Brand Should Have A Focus

If you are building a personal brand that tries to cater to the needs of every member of an industry, the brand is going to be overwhelmed. Once your brand is overwhelmed, it is bound to fail. Your brand should have a target demographic, and your brand message should focus on this demographic.

By focusing on this demographic, it is easier to create content to meet the needs of your audience. Another benefit of being focused is that your brand becomes specific. A specific brand understands what it needs to offer as well as the best way to present what it has to offer.

Be Authentic

Being authentic is something that happens naturally for a personal brand. You are more likely going to fail when you try to paint an image that is not an accurate reflection of you. An authentic brand is a personal brand with a voice that aligns with the actions it takes.

Managing a personal brand is much easier when you are authentic. Why? You don't have to worry about changing your personality every time you need to interact with your audience. If you must create a fake online persona to build a personal brand, you should remember that you may also have to interact with your audience in-person at one point.

Your Brand Should Have A Story

To build a successful personal brand, you must have a great story to tell and also be an excellent storyteller. People want to interact with the narrative of your personal brand.

Storytelling will help your audience connect with the brand on an emotional level. As much as people love a good story, no one wants a boring story. You can present your brand story in the form of a video or as written content.

Some critical elements of a great brand story include who you are, why you are building a personal brand and your brand values. Your story should depict your struggles from the initial stages to where you are now.

Your Brand Should Be Consistent

Consistency in personal branding implies that your brand should stick to a strategy and follow-through repeatedly. If you decide to build a brand in the fitness industry, ensure the content you create relates to fitness. You can create a post on fitness today, and tomorrow you can populate your pages with content related to entrepreneurship.

Your consistency should also affect your brand both online and off-fline. Through consistency, you can get your audience to trust in your brand since they know what to expect from the brand. Don't confuse your audience just because you are desperate to get views, likes, or comments.

Consistency covers more than just the content. Basic activities like posting daily quotes counts. If you have been posting daily motivational quotes on your pages, you need to continue doing so. Most members of your audience will be looking forward to the next quote.

Have A Mentor

A mentor is simply someone that has been in your current position and can give you tips to guide you to success. When building a personal brand, connecting with other people that have made successful personal brands is a great way to grow your brand. These individuals can give you pointers and tell you some of the things you need to avoid when building your personal brand.

You can also follow successful individuals like celebrities and top in-fluencers within your industry. Learn how they interact with their au-dience. Are there things you are doing wrong? What strategies can you implement? These are some easy ways to ensure the success of your personal brand.

Using Data and Analytics

Success in your personal branding should be something you bring about using facts and figures. You cannot will a personal brand to success. There are various data and analytical tools available in as-sessing the growth of a personal brand to determine where you can make improvements.

In addition to the tools that have been specially designed for analyti-cal purposes, most social media platforms also feature their unique data and analytics tool for users to utilize. These tools let you keep track of specific metrics that determine the performance of your branding strategy on the platform.

Depending on how the social media platform operates, there will be some unique metrics that you can assess. Understanding a platform is essential if you intend to optimize the available analytics tools fully.

Facebook offers an analytics tool in the form of Facebook Insights. Insights gives access to post-level and page-level metrics. The post-level metrics includes the likes, comments, reach, shares, and refer-ral traffic the page is getting. The page-level metrics include page fan growth, video metrics, engagement rate, conversions, and page views.

Twitter analytics also offers both page-level metrics and post-level metrics. Page-level metrics on the Twitter includes profile visits and follower growth while post-level metrics includes tweet impressions, replies, retweets, likes, and referral traffic. There is an analytics button which is accessible from the dashboard of your Twitter account.

To assess the performance of your Instagram personal branding strategies, you may need to use an external tool. Nonetheless, you should still look out for metrics such as likes, comments, total followers, and clicks on the account.

Analytics also applies to your other channels including your YouTube channel, blog, LinkedIn profile, and website.

Tailoring Your Content to A Growing Audience

As your personal brand keeps growing, you will keep experiencing an influx of new followers on your various social media channels. You need to keep posting content that will be relevant to both your existing and new audience to remain successful. It is crucial you interact with the audience regularly to find out the type of content they need.

Chapter 12:
Become the Next Million Dollar Brand

Society is steadily breaking away from the norm. The norm in which an individual goes to college, gets a degree, and then lands a dream job. The current framework that society is slowly shaping into is one where everyone has the power to make a difference.

The main tool for bringing about this change is personal branding. Personal branding is changing the way things are being done both in our interaction with other individuals as well as with businesses. Through social media, everyone now has the power to leverage their influence in getting what they truly desire. It may be getting a job, growing a business, or attracting more customers.

By implementing the various strategies in this book, you can get ahead in your goal of building a personal brand. Building a personal brand is a process that requires a lot of time investment. Nonetheless, your investments in form of time, money, and effort usually pays off if you are patient and determined.

Looking at the trends when building a personal brand is always beneficial if you go about it in the right manner. Implementing a new idea just because it is the current trend can lead to failure if it is not something you are passionate about. Therefore, you need to focus on your area of expertise when developing your personal brand.

If your main goal is to make money through personal branding, chasing this goal blindly will not get you to any favorable position. A lot of personal brands that follow this pattern often end up failing because they do not have anything unique to offer their audience.

There have been lots of individuals that have created very successful personal brands. The strategies these individuals followed on their road to success are all similar and this book covers all these strategies and more. If you want to become the next million-dollar brand, then you need to start implementing everything you have learned in this book.

For each strategy you implement on a social media platform, remember to use the analytics tool in assessing your performance. Hope will not grow your personal brand. Using data and analyzing each area of your strategy will yield tangible results.

While you can become very successful through personal branding on social media, you also need to remember that consistency and authenticity play a vital role. Don't try to copy other personal brands to create a shortcut to success.

Wyatt Croasdell

"Short cuts make long delays." — J.R.R. Tolkien, The Fellowship of the Ring.

If you find this book helpful in anyway a review to support my endeavors is much appreciated.

Influencer Brand in The Digital Age

Wyatt Croasdell